I0843050

BE NICE

KAREN KELLOCK PH.D.

**Manual for
Superior Men**

**A complete theory based on Einstein physics,
Political Psychology, Systems Theory
and Archetypal Psychiatry.**

FORMULA

**All success attraction
All disease obstruction
All recovery elimination**

**You must fast on all three
OBSTRUCTIONS:
People
Habit
Food**

BE NICE

The bible calls it a DROUGHT: when no one knows what you're talking about--spiritual and mental nuts.   The female community is a massive impediment to genius: they are petty, mean, underhanded, fiendish. They hang together like peas in a pod and gossip [like old hens going for recognition] that you're odd.   The calumny is horrible and unwarranted. Just cuz one says something they take it as truth darn it.

BE NICE

KIDS RULED BY TEMPLATES
THEY WANT WHAT THEY WANT
NARCISSIST DISCARDER OR JUST TIRED?
WE ALL ACTED ATTROCIOUSLY
SOLITUDE-THRIVERS SEEN AS HATERS
IS SPOUSE A FENCE OR A HOOVER?
SYSTEMS TRIGGER BRAIN CHEMICALS
WHAT TO DO NOW THEY'RE HERE
ATTRACTIONS TO UNMET NEEDS
WHEN YOU GET RID OF LOSERS
CHASE THE TRUE SELF ONLY
I WANT PROTECTION!
EXPECT LONELINESS [BLISS]
LONELINESS IS DISCONNECTION FROM SELF
WOMEN'S STUDIES: STITCH OR BITCH?
IT'S THE STYLE TO BASH MEN
IMPLOSION OF WHITE WEST
ENCUMBRANCE OF OFFICIOUS SOCIAL WORLD
POPULARITY OF HUMAN CONSTRUCTIONS
HUMAN INTERACTION CAN BE BORING
YOUR TIME IS THEIRS TO WASTE
NEVER BORED OR LONELY
SOLUTUDE GAINS
THEY'RE BORED CUZ THEY HAVE NO LIFE
I CAN'T TALK I GOTTA WORK
DON'T GET SOCIAL WHEN LONELY
OF COURSE IT'S ATTRACTION
WARPED SIGNALS, CUES AND TRIGGERS
DEALING WITH TOXIC PEOPLE
SOCIAL INVASIONS/FRIENDS OF FRIENDS
FALLING TO LOWER. COMPANIONS
MOST ENERGETIC GETS MOST WARPED
EFFECTS OF BAD ASSOCIATES
SEE ANGER AS A SPECTRUM
THE ANGER-PRONE DON'T HAVE THE TOOLS

BE NICE

REPETITION COMPULSIONS
VIOLATION OF PERSONAL STANDARDS!
YOU'RE A SPONGE OF GROSS INVADERS
HANGOUT CULTURE WASTES TIME
SOCIAL TYRANNY GET AWAY FROM ME
BEHAVIOR HAS CONSEQUENCES GOOD/BAD
DON'T FILL MY HOUSE WITH YOUR FRIENDS
ONLY A GENIUS SEES GENIUS
CHILDHOOD PTSD
WHAT IS A REAL MAN?
ADDICTIVE DEVICES TO COMPENSATE
DYSREGULATION AND ADDICTION
BACK INTO THE PORN TROUGH
NOT GONNA FALL APART AGAIN
HIS DO-NOTHING SPIRIT
HAVE YOU BECOME A DETECTIVE?
SWEET MEAN CYCLE
THEY CRAVE EXCITEMENT
INCENTIVE GONE, WIND FALLS COME
ATTACHMENT STYLE: APPROACH-AVOIDANCE
MAINTAIN FALSE IDENTITY
NARCS HAVE NO EMPATHY
NO COMPROMISE TRUTH FOR PROMISE
TRAUMA BOND SYMPTOMS
NEVER REAL APOLOGIES
NO WEIRD STUFF!
MOMMY SOFT PORN AND JERRY SPRINGER
NO NUDES/X LANGUAGE BUT STILL GARBAGE
OLD MEN'S BRAIN CONDITION AND SEX
FLAKY NO-SHOWS
BANISH NO-SHOW FLAKES
BOUNDARY-BUSTERS
THEY'LL IMPOSE IF YOU LET EM
SILENT TREATMENT

BE NICE

EFFECT OF SILENT TREATMENT ON CHILD
LEAVE THE SNAKE PIT
THEY DIDN'T HONOR YOUR "NO"
LIBERALS HAVE DIRTY MINDS
PORN IS CHEATING
PORN DEMORALIZATION WEAPON
CODEPENDENCY OR VICTIM?
DON'T CRAPFIT EVIL OFFSHOOTS
BE YOUR OWN SOCIAL ENGINEER
HIX POLITIX
STUPID STUFF BY STUPID PEOPLE
SPORTSBALL IS ALL
BOTOX AND OTHER DAM SCAMS
DON'T GET ON THAT WHEEL
GRATITUDE IS AN OPENER
THERE IS NOTHING IN THEIR HEAD
THE END
HOW TO RID TOXIC MEMORY
THAT OLD ERA ERASED IN HISTORY
GOD A DANGEROUS ENEMY OF SIN
INVASION INTO ISOLATION
PH.D D IN THE STREETS
ARCHETYPICAL LEVELS
RECAP ON LIBERAL AREAS
HEALTHY MINDEDNESS
EAT AS THEY DID IN HISTORY
EUROPE: BAKERY THEN FISH
MAKING YOU SICK THRU MEALS
FORGET DIET DOGMA JUST FAST
EAT WHAT/ALL YOU WANT THEN FAST
SATEITY POWER NOT VITAMINERALS
GLOBAL BLOCKS TO SUCCESS

BE NICE

The bible calls it a **DROUGHT**: when no one knows what you're talking about--spiritual and mental nuts.

Tho' I live in beauty/tranquility I still feel like a cat in a roomful of rocking-chairs due to my memories.

The constant pressure from untrained kids who want what you have and they've absolutely **NO** brakes.

After all that nothing was more important than my dignities and boundaries, cross-reinforcing.

The female community is a massive impediment to female genius: they are petty, mean, underhanded, fiendish.

They hung together like peas in a pod and gossiped [like old hens going for recognition] that I was odd.

The calumny was horrible and unwarranted. Just cuz one said something they took it as truth darnit.

KIDS RULED BY TEMPLATES

Just cuz I didn't fit their high school template of how one should **BE** and **THINK** I was their target.

And this went on until I got married then it all stopped suddenly. Marriage is a fence honey.

Marriage is a magic carpet ride as you fly away from all you've known and **TO** a wonderful new land.

I will always want to be married. I will never want that big bull's eye painted on me again, harried.

Marriage is freedom for a woman, not a. cage like the old hag feminists say like Steinem and Friedan.

BE NICE

I can work **ALL DAY AND NIGHT** unobstructed cuz I got a guard in his man cage ready to block it.

Cuz in this world there's a conspiracy against a woman working in private--they expect her to listen up.

Yes they hurt me but that was my Ph.D. in the Streets teaching me how to be/how to stay **FREE**.

Don't bemoan past mistakes [being taken by fakes] cuz to get to here--magnificent--it takes what it takes.

I've been married for 13 years of freedom, before that it was a bedlam of confusion in worldly collisions.

They'd take it as an obvious insult when I'd react: "why are you bothering me?"--then I'd be in for it.

In social generations genius and the True Self is hard to illuminate--to develop inwardly brings bad fate.

They fight it: time for yourself, living your own schedules, refusing to adapt to anyone. They **HATE THIS**.

To be a genius discoverer you must **MAKE YOUR OWN MAP: TODAY**, or must you adapt to **THAT**?

THEY WANT WHAT THEY WANT

They want you to do what **THEY** do and think what **THEY** think and nothing else is legit to these finks.

Get your own life before it's too late. If caught early enough you can make some real money this way.

For that True Self is the pearl hard to find but inside is a kernel of rare **GENIUS**--knowing you're own mind.

It doesn't come from being **NICE** to people [tho' we should] but finding the true self, understood?

BE NICE

I prayed God would give me something to do so He put a Creative Act inside me and it took decades too.

Van Gogh and Gauguin argued constantly about painting. I don't like community, I'd rather be solo writing.

STYLE. It's universally recognized--what is it? Is it inborn or can you learn it? It's an archetype I think.

If it's two artists it's two houses, period. There's no way you can adapt and create content too I said.

NARCISSIST DISCARDER OR JUST TIRED?

Is he a narcissist discarder or are you an uninteresting clinger when he'd rather not linger?

Harry's run by his older wife. She's the leftist feminist who's gotten him like this, whipped.

Just like Jezebel and her flying monkey Johns, a whipped husband can be goaded into anything hon'.

He fell outa love due to her casual attitude about sex: "we worked it thru" she said of her male friends.

A casual attitude about sex belies inner bankruptcy: a seared conscience of a disgusting personality.

She gets on the stand to screw the "abusive" man while cryin' and then she wins cuz it's these times.

The jerk would drop in on me in the mornings right when I was planning my day--too high a price to pay.

Ok you learned your lessons now forget it. Don't let em hurt you twice: then doing it/you thinking about it.

How I'd handle it now: 1. The herb's not here, I keep it elsewhere. 2. Nobody gets in the house, they steal.

BE NICE

Remove the magnet, rid of maggots. Oh to be young again armed with these little wisdom nuggets.

Instead of bemoaning past resentments how about self-congratulating cuz you learned your lesson?

That's it, I'm not going to your page again cuz it's too confusing and besides I got my own thing.

I made it too much about your thing, it hung on in memory and I don't have the time for these chicaneries.

So goodbye and good luck. What the heck in ten years we may both be dead and I've a time budget.

I'm facing heaven when ALL things I've known are dissolved like a vapor like they never occurred.

How you acted, heck how I acted--controlled by demons and forces before I learned my urgent lessons.

WE ALL ACTED ATTROCIOUSLY

How I acted was despicable and atrocious--controlled by outside forces, because I was weak in lowness.

How you acted was the same, despicably lame playing violent games. Separation was the solution: ok.

How to deal with PTSD memories: Record over the old tape with exciting substitutes [but I'm a recluse].

My biggest imposer and mischief-maker kept saying how "good" he was yet he robbed me blind alas.

Inside I hear women yelling at me and me raging at others--what'd happen if I were drinking?

They knew nothing about me other than my glaring differences from them--a dire situation.

BE NICE

I'm sick of politics, now it's movies music and other magic mental transports into higher realms, not lunatics.

I'm catering to my broken traumatized child inside. What would she want with that dirty ol' guy?

What I want is **STABILITY**: daddy, someone who's gonna keep my head above water and routines going.

A husband is **PROTECTION** so you can do your own thing within walls of safety and security: **LIBERTY**.

So I'm withdrawing from this situation which was only fantasyland: it's **END** is my new **BEGINNING**.

I just want protection to do my own thing, don't you get it man? Don't make it so complicated, scram.

SOLITUDE-THRIVERS SEEN AS HATERS

In the future I may need your suffocating help but for right now it's just an encumbrance, I must rebuff.

Besides, I found someone else to fawn over and think about. He's more attendant and not a louse.

I get the theory, we **DISTRACT** from core pain. Yep, I'm on the computer 20 hours a day distracting.

Any savant isolate is going to be constantly angry with social expectations and for this they hate him.

They hated my mother who was a genius who wanted to be alone. She was **ALWAYS** angry at them.

She wanted to build houses and empires and they wanted to pull her down through social expectations.

It was the 80s before computers: social expectations were like a religion like it's God you're worshippin'

BE NICE

You're too complicated in bad location with too many interrelations plus a huge fan base, no thanks.

Very debauched too, saying how many women you've had--I would think you'd be ashamed of that lad.

It's 3 am, gotta go feed dogs down the street raw meat cuz their dam mistress wants to keep em mean.

If you don't go to his page, he doesn't exist. Think about that miss, it ends all your pain that persists.

You got Jenna and Trevor your youtube mentors and all your pets surrounding you as loving supporters.

It was my first alcoholic husband throwing me to the wolves by inviting the kid thugs in for tacos.

IS SPOUSE A FENCE OR A HOOVER?

He was not only NOT a wall, he was a HOOVER of outside evils into the home and I had no protection.

This is not the fifties--there are dire evils out there and the home is the ONLY protection darn you.

He brought EVIL into my house and I had no defense! Of course I have PTSD from an alcoholic louse.

Just by listening to your channel I'm bringing evil into the house again. It's a spirit/you're not my friend.

The narcissist thinks you're an extension of him. That's why it's so painful in the discard phase I guess.

Who needs this? Not after discovering my inner realm in solitude: God, angels & ELEMENTS in total bliss.

I've written seven pages on how much you hurt me but I overcame it and came out BETTER, see.

BE NICE

I will not **SUBSTITUTE** thoughts of you with him instead. He's cuter and cares what I think in my head.

The mere fact you went thru that **PROVES** you still had to learn the lesson, so stop remembering all that.

SYSTEMS TRIGGER BRAIN CHEMICALS

Systems trigger brain chemicals like drugs so of course there's lunacy in families so forget it honey.

So it's **YOU--YOU'RE** the reason I've had self-esteem problems lately! I've removed the tumor finally.

The brain chemicals bring on misbehaviors cued from the deep collective unconscious, few know this.

It's dirty--it's **PEOPLE** worship and I'm not gonna participate in it. We're all flawed and you know it.

No politix just music cuz that's what the animals prefer. Don't be inconsiderate to your friends in fur.

I can hear women yelling at me. These are past events I blotted out at the time just to feel liberty.

So you can use it as a platform to shame me, make a point, rub it in, misadvise, make jealous? Hell no.

They've been told to be nice, which is "good". But that only comes from a healed personality not falsehood.

When I was nice they nearly destroyed me, my future, my home. I'll never be nice again just a good friend.

Faking nice will always come out sometime. Irritability, rough answers, deception, opacity, no shine.

If you put em on a pedestal, you're lower on the totem poll. If you're chasing you're not the star in your own cameo.

BE NICE

If you're just a cameo in someone else's they can feel that and want you just to let em do their lead role.

The reason is you're not at your own core. If you were, you'd be the star/you wouldn't be chasing him/her.

Why did I ever allow this person in my life? Looking back that is the question of a life filled with strife.

You gotta stop being so nice and instead set boundaries and MAJOR filters: men or mice?

WHAT TO DO NOW THEY'RE HERE

But now it's too late, they're here. What to do now? Don't engage them--let that be your policy, dear.

If you engage em mentally/physically/verbally it becomes mudslinging and since they're lower you're the victim.

Having a policy of non-reaction to toxic people calms you as the rabble settles down.

Whatever you do, always know: don't feed into the negativity because it creates a cyclone.

Instead of judging the miscreants [a TRAP] use em as a mirror to improve yourself fast [new map].

TIP: You always wanna be focused on yourself not judge other people cuz that backfires soon--and a lot.

Let toxic people be important reminders for you of your own areas of weakness or doing wrong.

Recap on toxic people: Either cut em off or minimize their effects cuz if you don't your life is hexed.

No one to blame but yourself for those attracted in. Why else did you attract juvenile delinquents?

BE NICE

With unmet needs you attract those who FILL the need but it's sick since those needs are only met in childhood.

You can't be validated externally--the external locus of control--but you will be exploited until you're old.

The undeveloped are a magnet to "advisor" types with the superior need to be dominant, but yikes!

ATTRACTIONS TO UNMET NEEDS

Advisors get a self-esteem boost too by twisting everything around to where they're advising you.

If chasing someone else you're externalizing your own happiness and if you take advice you're a mess.

If you're already whole and complete your vibration stops all this but unmet needs from the past attract it.

Once the rejected chaser becomes the heroine of her own movie the other starts seeing her as groovy.

The system becomes an interplay of vibrations based on our qualifications: wholeness or neediness?

When they energetically feel you don't need em anymore it's like a radar and instantly you're their star.

Chasing him to be in his movie comes from a lack mentality like you're not enough and what a turnoff.

The minute you stop chasing you start getting to your core. Like magic there's so much mystery there.

I'm sorry to tell you this but your blatant neediness is the most unattractive quality you have Miss.

Cuz when you reach your core you'll be doing things you're so impassioned about: your true energy and more.

BE NICE

WHEN YOU GET RID OF LOSERS

When I got rid of losers/users I was so enraptured with my own mind I started each new day at midnight!

That's what you want: your own thing, your DESTINY. And you'll know it for you were born to do it, easily.

These social losers of the new age will keep you from it. These Drip Dry Hangers just wanna hangout.

And what do they talk about? NOTHING. They are wasting your precious time. Prefer **WORKING** over talking.

When Mike the useless debater calls to see me I say "Why? I wanna work not talk and we'll NEVER agree."

It reminds me of Einstein who never bothered anyone, just did his work—men would travel days just to irk.

They just wanna argue, obstruct and misadvise. 99% of the people in your life may be an encumbrance.

As Uncle George always said, "don't rush the end": don't get impatient in a mad drive to completion.

For only calm patience [letting the Creative Act unfold naturally as part of nature] reveals its essence.

As we rescue ourselves from neediness we attract the appropriate since we always attract what we are.

We attract what we ARE, not what we SAY we are. Gravity doesn't fall down but TOWARDS: Affinitization.

I'm not saying I was always a saint or perfect. But as I face heaven or hell I try to do the right thing now.

All I know is life is short and wasted time is a crime cuz God gave us a destiny--before our birth it was designed.

BE NICE

Finding this destiny will bring you more joy and wholeness than anyone or anything but most never think of it.

Is it Meghan and Harry's new production company doing films on climate change? Hell no! Take a stand.

False narratives, false goals from being pawns of globalist plans of total tyranny cuz we're so nice, you see.

CHASE THE TRUE SELF ONLY

If you're chasing someone else it means that person is running--that's implied. Stop this or die.

Chasing people implies lack, neediness and resistance. I couldn't help it I never respected em, not a chance.

I was needy, so I gave him food and rest. I was needy, so I made him feel important and the very best.

Chasing implies you're not good enough already and you NEED someone else urgently, it's pathetic really.

Find yourself/stop this stuff and mass attractions are immediate. You want gravity--things chasing you, see?

Until you feel complete you'll put someone else on the pedestal--getting them is what makes you whole.

So you must see your own worth to stop chasing or flirt. YOU are the star not them--as God's boy/girl.

American architecture will be more like Mexicos: the fence, the gate, the wall is the most important, MOST.

American architecture was very social: big porches, front door right on the street and often no wall at all.

I WANT PROTECTION!

BE NICE

I wanna wall, a front yard and an atrium between me and them. This is 2020 and I want **PROTECTION**.

This "nice" thing has gotta go. It's ended our world as we are being replaced as if we're completely dispensable.

We feel sorry for people giving everything we own to them. What our ancestors left to us is going to bums.

"Nice" is the most dangerous concept ever. The heart is wicked, men are evil and none are good whatsoever.

Whoever delights in solitude is either a wild beast or a god. Anonymous

EXPECT LONELINESS [BLISS]

What you're doing when self-actualizing is rising above the vulgar, common masses--so expect loneliness.

The people around you are hooked to lower/common ways of doing things and misconceptions: conformists.

Your changes go beyond their comfort zones. They don't like being shown they're lazy/negligent ya' know.

Your nice new good example throws theirs into focus and it really sticks in their craw that you could do this.

Suddenly you see the cost of personal development as it makes people stay away. Some give it all up, ok?

Real growth requires turning inwards. You can know that but most of us are still concerned with the outers.

If on the hero's journey to be a leader, visionary or sage you must face issues of being alone/not hiding from this.

DUPED: As I found out thru years of trying, you can't raise your consciousness through a group.

BE NICE

It doesn't work thru groups. To grow you must enter the belly of the whale, go deep inside all by yourself.

You must face inner demons all by yourself not your friends--drip dry hangers keep you on the outer.

LONELINESS IS DISCONNECTION FROM SELF

LONELINESS is disconnection from the True Self or sin--cuz once whole you're never bored/lonely again.

It was exhilarating to realize solitude was my CENTER--that I was highest basking in my being undisturbed.

SOLITUDE is the bedrock of your being and you always return to it to get back your compass. YES!

You don't have to become a hermit, just face the issue-- seriously, then draw boundaries to prevent abuse.

Older people who haven't faced loneliness hang on even more to their friends as they fear being less.

There is no strength in groups, they hold you down. You must face that in the universe you are all alone.

When you're truly connected to God and the True Self you're never lonely. There's a beauty to it, truly.

The reason you're the hero is you've faced inner demons alone. ALONE: and that's how the hero's shown.

If you went to college to mimic your professor's views then your parents were dam fools to pay for your school.

When I think university I am shocked by the decline in serious knowledge and especially what's put in it's place.

It is no longer dispassionate inquiry [which fascinated me in school] but ideological conformity called "cool".

BE NICE

Ideology/pseudoscience have not yet triumphed. There's a backlash against college rot and it's giant.

WOMEN'S STUDIES: STITCH OR BITCH?

Women's Studies: Do they teach em how to stitch or bitch? I find them irrelevant/just anti-patriarchy.

There is no more critical reflection, but ideological dogmatism which is required of the young.

The biggest reason to sequester yourself is their constant ageist or officious comments pulling you down.

You're at your peak, you've got more to give than ever--just as they make ageist comments blocking clever.

You can't have this. You must see thru these people and break contact for the time is late and you're the best.

It's a tragic cosmic joke: Here you're better than ever just as they say you're over the hill, obsolete or whatever.

Now you're gonna have to buckle down to prove them all wrong--requiring all you've learned in a new song.

People just wanna hang out and waste your time--it's theirs to waste! Don't cave in cuz you're alone in any case.

Losers get a little bored or restless and use you as a pit stop. Don't allow this--tell em all to call FIRST.

Don't allow loser drop-ins to bring their friends. In social culture you aren't allowed to vet--a dangerous trend.

I've never gone to anyone's house--I'm too involved in my own--but those without a life will live thru yours alone.

They don't make their home into an otherworldly atmosphere, tidy and neat, happy and replete.

BE NICE

They got stuff everywhere, here and there helter-skelter, a sickening place to be. This is key.

IT'S THE STYLE TO BASH MEN

Women bash men, talk over you in a conversation, flirt with other men on a date and get mad at stupid stuff.

Feminist mom beat her son to death cuz he refused to dress like a girl--it's liberal tyranny in our world.

Most people skim the surface of life and miss 99% of the beauty that's there-- they're ordinary, not rare.

Most had an unhealthy trust that things would always the same so they were unprepared for what came.

After time alone we get into the simplicity of being but also the PROFUNDITY of being with miracles seen.

I became enraptured with solitude, every minute was so fascinating and when people came, I stewed.

I could still interact with people ["social"] but it was so much less than this ecstasy I became a no-show.

I saw the social as insane. Kissing, hugging, going along, conforming but telling the truth brought shame.

Social drop-ins were pure aggravation. I told them to call first next time but when they did I didn't want em.

The social world is pure inanity and dullness. I turned down all invitations from then on, I wanted only FULLNESS.

Suddenly the social was missing completely but that was ok, I just craved solitude and it was 100% soon.

When safely in solitude you see social niceties as crazies smiling to get approval from peanut galleries.

BE NICE

My sleep pattern changed. I was up all night and felt a new bliss being separate from the modern/deranged.

IMPLOSION OF WHITE WEST

The white-built West was imploding with these invasions so I wanted separation from diversity promulgations.

I took on personal development and self-actualization as my mission in life. Just with God = no more strife.

My own inner journey was the CORE of my life and everything else like friends was a mere tangent.

They began to criticize me for being anti-social or without friends--a hideous stigma but I stayed on this trend.

I would take long desert walks, thrilled to be one with nature all alone--it was boring with others along.

I found there was nothing I could do with others that wasn't better alone, in fact it was the opposite--so be gone!

My entire life was resistance to chaos created by others. I was miserable 'til I said "don't come here, EVER".

At this time I found my life purpose. It was to write these words after experiencing this people chaos.

The only reason others don't feel this: they've mal-adapted to chaos while needing other people as crutches.

The bad advice from interlopers cost me highly in money, time and integrity. Now it's an evil spirit to me.

Now I choose my counselors carefully but firstly I listen to my insides along with prayerful study/scrutiny.

Losers drop in to people's houses. Winners are so busy working they wouldn't think of this/no allowances.

BE NICE

It was a madhouse trying to keep people away so we relocated and I'm happily in solitude today.

ENCUMBRANCE OF OFFICIOUS SOCIAL WORLD

This was my WAR: Learning about myself, my limitations and the encumbrance of the officious social world.

Ms. Social Charm always has cars parked at her house. In and out all day they come and go, a giant farce.

I detested modern social customs of women always kissing each other--is this gay grooming I wondered?

Facelift: Do it once and that's it. Injections: have to do it thrice a year--more chemicals shot under the skin.

My only answer was to live a contemplative lifestyle: the mode of the philosopher/thinker was my style.

Not socializing, not being seen, not taking endless selfies for all to see but a discoverer interested in eternity.

I constructed my life according to existence itself--the elements--not according to human constructs.

This new view brought tremendous backlash. They called me crazy and antisocial but I just loved the elements.

Sound of rain on my cabin's tin roof: It was so enchanting then there'd be a door knock from some goof.

They'd talk incessantly: boring, irrelevant and aggravating. I asked em to leave saying "I got family coming".

They hated me for staying separate from expectations of society--something they couldn't do apparently.

26 years in a tiny cabin taught me how to draw boundaries and insist on privacy as a constitutional right, see?

BE NICE

The lost can't relate to this since they cling to human crutches thinking that's all they have as such.

Social generations sees this as criminal, rude and mental while I saw them as rude/imposing/ungentle.

POPULARITY OF HUMAN CONSTRUCTIONS

Human constructions [like entertainment] are very popular but flimsy ya' know--they come and go.

Like all human obstructions they are EGO-obstructions and ferociously defended, as in: "you must come".

Human constructions always become political in power struggles, greed, fear, competition between egos.

All the dark elements of the ego come into this. You must conform to them or it's an unacceptable DIS.

Women were the worst enforcers. Even the churches would bother me as if I was slapping em in the face.

America is about individual identity but the social world only holds together thru forced conformity.

It was more important that I make a show than whether I got anything out of it--it's all about image ya' know.

They'd say "come on--it'll do you good". I learned to say "I'll decide that not you, just cuz you think I should".

I became so aggravated with society's interruptions I married a loner in two separate houses on land.

Spouse must be someone who loves privacy just as much. Such people aren't cold, they can love a bunch.

Being out in nature always brought great relief--cuz it's innocent and not ego-driven like the energy thief.

BE NICE

Being in nature and looking out to eternity was innocent, loving, godly, inspiring, revealing, mind-opening.

HUMAN INTERACTION CAN BE BORING

Being with humans was aggravating, boring, irritating, pointless, mind-raping and discouraging.

City scholars would ask to come out and debate me. Why? Unsure of their reality but I just wanted to BE.

Read the books if you want to know but as for me, I just wanna BE. No more useless debates, I'm free.

Constructions are all ego, delusion and B.S. They're not eternal and change constantly, please notice this.

I loved being out in nature so they'd wanna come along. INSTANTLY it's magic and mystery was gone.

Nonsense, manipulation and doubletalk: once free it was a phantasmagoria of excitement around the clock.

And the human manipulations--I vowed for the rest of my life to move away from these obstructions.

When we got to the new place the neighbors wanted to swoop us up in their net but we saw the threat.

Losers sitting around talking, divorced from Self. Their center is entirely social and there's NOTHING else.

As I released ego/moved away from ego it was reflected in my surroundings and I was good to go/ready to show.

As long as I was around them I was encrusted with superfluity--it reflected in frustration and ugly.

Only free was I pretty. For social mal-adaptations reflect on the face in frown lines, anger and worry.

BE NICE

Did you ask them to come, or are you constantly adapting to their rude interruptions? Question this chum.

YOUR TIME IS THEIRS TO WASTE

In the social world your time is their's to waste. These are losers without a life, they don't care about "space".

The monastic life is simplified and being alone is much simpler than being with the herd of conformers.

Alone, you get the deepest connection to reality so it's far more fulfilling. Prove this to yourself: let em in.

Even if you're an extrovert, the deepest issues in life are confronted head-on ALONE. I want it, be gone.

I developed strategies to maximize this life: I took ten-day solo retreats--no traveling just sitting in my seat.

No cell phones, no technology, no going to the door: just me being with myself for ten days or more.

NEVER BORED OR LONELY

At first loneliness seems like torture but soon the inner realm alights and it's heavenly bliss for sure.

Once I passed day 7 there was a shift in me. I passed that hump and broke thru to the beauty of simply being.

Ensconced in loneliness I was never so happy in my life. The neediness for people was gone along with strife.

Just from sitting alone on my couch I grew so much. I shot up spiritually/loved myself as God gave me hunches.

After this switch there was a giant backlash as people were horrified I didn't need em a bunch like all the rest.

BE NICE

Since then I've come to see this as a big deal. Social transcends personal autonomy in the era of sex appeal.

All day long there are cars in and out of her parking lot. It's all an outer journey to rot not an inner one to God.

Forget new age books, just be alone for ten days to discover yourself while revealing those crooks.

Stop saying you're such a "good person". Jesus said NO one is good even Him--only God is good, amen.

My intruder kept calling himself "good" but then stole little things outa the house like a dam hood.

SOLUTUDE GAINS

I grew more than I ever did in years. It was like waking up to the stars and seeing abundance everywhere.

It was near-impossible to break my ten-day people fast. Food I need but people? Yes, I guess they're nice.

It separated me from familial beginnings/prejudices as well as cultural modes as they constantly re-adjust.

I escaped the enforced conformities from 1990-2006 and I'm so glad I did. I seemed like an alien to the kids.

Forget reading endless books or even meditation. Just sit alone on your couch and go within.

Sitting in a lonely jail cell changed Paul. Many go crazy cuz they don't realize it's a spiritual opportunity/call.

Intruders irritated for they hadn't broken through the cultural grime: nothing in common/different past-times.

It was near-impossible to break my ten-day people fast. Food I need but people? Yak, yak, yak all gas.

BE NICE

TRY it, you'll love it. Stop being a pit stop and prevent people from using you as entertainment.

New Age teachings for fifty years have removed all structure and now there is only purposeful disorder.

THEY'RE BORED CUZ THEY HAVE NO LIFE

They're bored cuz they have no inner life--all outer chit chat--so they use you then fill you with strife.

I challenged my neighbor to a ten-day people fast and she panicked at the thought, choosing social emptiness.

I walked into the room of women and was kissed/hugged then mugged: I felt I couldn't say what I wanted.

If you take herbs to break thru, lean into those feelings of sadness, loneliness and then **BLISS** when through.

Now when I'm with friends and having fun it's icing on the cake, something I don't completely depend on.

They want me to go "out" with them. I never will because **NOTHING** out there is as fascinating as home.

So that's the Karen Kellock Recluse Theory and I can guarantee it will release **ALL** your misery.

My 26 years in desert solitude established a firm foundation for life, to return in mind with any strife.

I feel discordant or imposed on and I think of the mountains and desert walks and want them immediately gone.

People wreck your life and waste all your time. Don't let em--it's really the devil blocking destiny/rhymes.

I only want people who can do me some good. Backers, tech guys, advisors, encouragers not losers/users.

BE NICE

You've come so far. Don't wreck it now by who you let into your house: take these sagacious words to heart.

I CAN'T TALK I GOTTA WORK

All I hear myself saying is "sorry, I have to work" cuz it seems you're constantly interrupted in the universe.

I thank my interlopers for teaching me these wonderful life-saving lessons so you could benefit from them.

The social culture says doing things by yourself is wrong, weird or abnormal but it's the WAY to be a marvel.

Solo travel is a powerful way to connect to self/God and I'd do it were it not for the chemicals all around us.

You have to feel your emotions when you're alone, not distracting yourself, to escape social hell.

After he shortchanged you or something like that, never have that thief around again for regret it.

Get INTO your loneliness and let solitude massage you. It's the key to affluence/abundance for the recluse

After you've done this, cultivate suitable friendships and do something of value for the world which needs it.

You can do this now since solitude makes you SUPER creative. I write all day and night to make it.

Most importantly: solitude gives you the vision of a genius that most can/will never understand, honest.

Solitude gives you foresight/wisdom which you can draw on to give back to the world of fools and bums.

Even so, your new friendships/contributions to the world are secondary to what you've found inside girl.

BE NICE

They are secondary because you built this foundation from your solitude and that you will always return to.

DON'T GET SOCIAL WHEN LONELY

Don't do what most do: become more socially active when lonely. Depression happens, that's just too easy.

TV prompts us to have many friends and hangout all day. But they're after little fish, we're after the whale.

By hanging out all they do is get stuck in cultural ruts while we explore what life is **REALLY** all about.

Th whale is: finding your true self, the holy grail--and facing your inner demons from a past so stale.

When you have no one to talk to nor understand, remind yourself this is the most important thing to man.

Recap: We want to find the True Self created by God but groups and so-called friends will call you odd.

What you're doing here is personal development and it's a big thing! No one does it unless they wanna be king.

Is it tough or lonely at times? Hell yah but the benefits are so great it divides you from the slaves/old grind.

If it means you gotta look a little weird or crazy do it anyway. It's the Hero's journey all thru history.

Life is ALL you but in the social world that's fragmented and you can't see that--that's the problem ego.

And then we treat others like they can give us something--as if attention and approval gets us to the goal.

If you don't get this, all those useless things like approval you'll be chasing forever: remove em now.

BE NICE

You'll have down times on this path. Just keep reminding yourself it's the most important thing, you'll be glad.

OF COURSE IT'S ATTRACTION

Of COURSE it's attraction. If you wanna be a success, make yourself apt for success first, this is obvious.

It's not "attraction" in a law of affinity metaphysical sense, but finding yourself by removing the superfluous.

When I finally disentrenched from the system he started to "hoover" me again--suck me back into him.

The hooverer realizes the person he nonchalantly walked away from has gained strength/he wants her again.

Doing God's work makes you nothing, nit, zero, not a thing. But He repays you in other ways: wait and see.

I made NO money from a lifelong project but from other avenues God gave me plenty, a giant bounty.

Everyone's so concerned with Harry and Meghan not realizing they a marvelous destiny of their own.

You shouldn't cuddle with your fiance until you're properly married. It's licentious to do so, sleazy.

Cuddling is a NO-NO and between men? Rather disgusting and I couldn't believe it when they said it.

WARPED SIGNALS, CUES AND TRIGGERS

Signals/withdrawals in early childhood create a massive dys-synchrony of cues/triggers: just plain crazy.

Why do they call alcohol a "social lubricant"? Because you'd have to be drunk to go along with all this.

BE NICE

Don't let em tell you not to do your work cuz it doesn't make money--genius persevered all thru history.

The greatest masterpieces were unfinanced, they were just done as a structure in nature by the artist.

Many masterpieces unrecognized until after the artists' death--does it mean they shouldn't have done em?

"If it makes no money, junk it"--really? Should I have given up this lifelong project, feeling called as the Elect?

It was when I had matured enough that God gave me the cars, the clothes, the house and everything else.

Get off of the money thing, this is where faith comes in. If God told you to do it He'll supply it/I'm proof of it.

I'm not telling you to quit your good job/give up what is good--I would never do that, just trust God.

I can hear people yelling at me in my mind. This is probably mom and all the harridans since then/the unkind.

DEALING WITH TOXIC PEOPLE

Toxic people are negative environments which ruin your potential by wasting time/making you miserable.

If people are always dragging you down thru their constant pessimism and selfish meddling--don't let em in.

The schools sealed our self-destruction by preventing us from the protection of seeing good/bad divisions.

They're constantly feeding you limiting beliefs and perhaps anger the energy thief. When rid of em, great relief.

Seeing ALL as good and justifying their bad acts due to a bad childhood: danger for you/amnesty for hoods.

BE NICE

Remember, we're a **SPONGE**. We're soaking them all in--all their negativity, lowness and grunge.

It is the most sensitive and spiritual who tend to absorb up the most crap--they are designed for that.

SOCIAL INVASIONS/FRIENDS OF FRIENDS

I had no defenses when a visitor brought all his friends into my house. It was a flood of noise and chaos.

This period taught me more than a library of books and I have those thugs to thank for the proper outlook.

I came from a sheltered home where I was always busy and alone. I had no idea humans could go this low.

My psyche was wide open: to new insights and visions, but tremendously vulnerable to collapse with invasions.

I've had **PTSD** ever since invasion by kids. These weren't kids like the 1950's but debauched, lawless pigs.

The bible talks about children ruling over adults--where there is no discipline or respect but pure insult.

And to think those pigs are now in their fifties with kids of their own makes me know our civilization is done.

The writer has to work so hard to counteract their affects he finally fails for in this environment he mal-adapts.

Whenever viewing the **PERSON** we must see the **SYSTEM** surrounding him for astute psychological analyzing.

To understand the person we must reverse engineer everything. Work it back--never see in isolation.

Life is too short to deal with toxic people. Stop putting up with things until at age 60 you finally see the evil.

BE NICE

Effects of people go far deeper than most realize. On every level it's ruin as you're cut down to size.

Get approval and a smile, you're happy all day. But with disapproval you're miserable : what a life, hurray.

FALLING TO LOWER. COMPANIONS

When in addiction we always fall to lower companions. These are the frenemy liars encouraging your ruin.

They won't treat you right if rich and famous, they'll still bring you down by encouraging sin--shameless.

Life is already too challenging when developing--why bring yourself down with something so deadening?

But since we're told to be nice/loving, we put up with em thinking they won't do it again--they **WILL** lovey.

It is the nature of the beast. There are two things in life: good and evil and these people aren't best for you.

Being **NICE** will ruin your life.

And if you let em get away with it they'll come back twice as bad and throw you in a pit. You can count on it.

Joseph's own brothers tried to kill him/sell him into slavery. Our worst enemies are in our home God said to me.

Jesus came with a sword to **DIVIDE** not to unite. Unity churches are evil as can be, separation is the key.

All of our problems are due to our associates since as man adapts to his environment he gets messed up.

What's the reason for keeping em around? So you won't be alone--the very thing making you renowned.

BE NICE

Clean sweep: get rid of all of em. Cultivate friends who support, encourage and make you positive, amen.

I want friends who are building something WITH me rather than going against me: a true community.

MOST ENERGETIC GETS MOST WARPED

The more energy we're born with the more intensely we get wrapped up in sin. Watch this, go within.

The more energy, intensity and imagination you have the more potential to be enslaved to sin--imagine that.

Either these people will encourage you to sin or you'll sin just to cope with your "guests" in mal-adaptation.

Sin--missing the mark--is a mal-adaptive coping device. What are we coping with? Frenemies who are "nice".

Frenemies encourage you to sin or you'll sin just to cope with em. I'll say it again: put em in the trash bin.

So you're so reliant on social relationships you can't get rid of em. This is indeed your biggest problem.

It creates a Spiral of Negativity which drags you down, down, down until there's nothing left of your destiny.

That's why we live in two houses. It isn't him but my past conditioning by frenemies: lushes and louses.

I've often heard of Vietnam vets who had to be alone half the year even tho' happily married. This is a WAR.

It makes you nervous like a grenade range or ticking time bomb. Even in peace you're still that way, in sum.

It was I who did it to myself be letting em in--but that in itself was a mal-adaptation from when young.

BE NICE

EFFECTS OF BAD ASSOCIATES

You are the average of the top five associates you hangout with. Jim Rohn

If this is true, do you want positive empowering friends or negative disempowering people keeping you down?

Tally up the people you hangout with. You may be shocked to discover most of em as entirely negative.

It's like we hang into the relationship to change their views or finally get their encouragement. Give it all up.

I kept people around on a mission to convince em. Just like all neuroses is "correction" of a system when young.

She came from miserable, depressive anger-prone people. It was her goal to change em to not be so evil.

This is not a digression--I contend your success is blocked purely by your associations/coping with sins.

He's over there and you're here, no one comes to the door and you don't answer phones. NOW you can show.

To sort this out, look at the TYPES of people. The more intimate the relationship, the more effects of evil.

Family issues are the most sticky/thorny. So let's drill down to their effects, heal, then get on to our destiny.

Remember, anyone can be toxic. We tend to hang on to people we've known all our life, never examining it.

How badly do you want success: health and wealth? Decide that then proceed to exorcise the filth.

What is TOXIC? People who are depressed, those who are pessimistic [limiting] and the dogmatic closed-mind.

BE NICE

Most toxic: anger-prone, violent people. Just as you wouldn't let a rabid dog in, see it and reject evil.

SEE ANGER AS A SPECTRUM

SEE anger as a spectrum. From mildly annoyed at things to full-out violence with no self-control or discipline.

Never make excuses for that thinking you can calm him. it will happen again, don't ever let him back in.

Violent boys and men are rabid dogs: Entirely unpredictable--a haunted house without God.

Many young men are pre-convicts. They are primed for it as their feminist moms/grandmas never disciplined.

After he threw beer all over her wall and paintings she let him back in anyway, sure it was just an anomaly.

Violent women are just as bad and we're seeing this more each day. Bad mothers can be the most cruel, ok?

People don't know how to settle arguments anymore. Lacking thinking skills to debate they just roar.

I'm not over-interested in relationships, I see them as CENTRAL to why misery and sin persists.

When a liberal feminist female had tyranny over me I lost my mind. I was aggravated, sad, nervous all the time.

People say you should be able to overcome this while staying in the relationship. This is a lie, falseness.

The answer is neurophysiology. Cue-trigger-rewind, repetition compulsion: environment makes us crazy.

Environment made her sick/bad: As she desperately searched for the solution she fell into her bag.

BE NICE

Toxic environments trigger old habits long gone. This is where it's really bad since they're further along.

Pick up a drink after a decade of sobriety: it's progressed as if you never stopped and now it's deadly.

THE ANGER-PRONE DON'T HAVE THE TOOLS

The anger-prone may not have the TOOLS to rewire his computer. Recall this: violence is his only answer.

Murder was so rare it shocked the world. Now it happens ever minute, you must fence your boys and girls.

The next group is the DRAMATIC. It's always up and down, making mountains outa molehills, the over-reactive.

You want a rock. Someone who's levelheaded where you are not. Dramatics are outa grace as life turns to rot.

These people have a very turbulent and dramatic lifestyle and they love it. You can't have this and make it.

Just cuz they don't know the value of home--having never had one--you'll let em tear down yours? Think hon'

They are neurotic entirely wanting only to socialize/party. To find your destiny, God needs your receptivity.

Then there are those in criminal activity. This is really thorny even if unintentionally involved--please see.

Things that are shady, don't seem right, appear unethical or unconstitutional, seem ungodly: reject, be free.

If their life is upside down they'll be leeches on yours. You're not a fixit shop for thieves, dealers, whores.

My destiny is to intellectually release thee after my own creativity was hidebound by makers of misery.

BE NICE

People held me down for decades but are these lost, you say? No, cuz God wants me to talk about it, ok?

Held down by alcoholic mother, then by feminist sisters, then by alcoholic husband then by the vixens.

REPETITION COMPULSIONS

It's called **REPETITION COMPULSION** and the problem is those caught in it can't see why you hate em.

She now has a husband who doesn't drink or smoke but due to her warlike past he lives in the other house.

The victim of warlike narcissism feels like a cat in a roomful of rocking chairs. She may never get past it, ever.

To know what happened to me just read my Twitter feed. Tho' I experienced it, it isn't an autobiography.

Then there are those with addictions. Hardcore is obvious but what about video games, TV, trends/fashions?

Maybe they're addicted to food and wanna dine out all the time. That's a real problem too/a waste of time.

I now see restaurants as dirty traps but there was a time it was all I thought about. Being served, dining out.

What is the simple solution to all this? To cut people outa your life. It's so simple most miss it or take a pill.

Most never think of doing this, they just put up with it. Be a scalpel cutting out a rotten tumor, then success.

Because we are a sponge and tend to mimic the bums it **SEEPS** into our system then the cancer builds up.

First it infects your mind then habits, emotions, ways of thinking or disregarding: it colors your perspective.

BE NICE

You must have courage to simply cut em out of your life. Think: cut em out then life shoots up, free of lies.

VIOLATION OF PERSONAL STANDARDS!

If someone's violating your standards, principals and values in life then he should be cut--but obvious it's not.

It doesn't matter who it is. Friends, bosses, relatives, customers all alike: if they're unfit, dismiss.

But I can't cut my boss off or my oldest friend off. Yes you can if destiny/success comes with your breakoff.

You must accept that everyone can be cut. You must have boundaries as a human being to keep out nuts.

When you mature you have principals and you hold others to principals. Not as a stickler but a good feller.

So if someone violates an important principal to you, they get cut--but the closer they are the more it hurts.

Even if it's your parents or children, you still gotta have boundaries or you'll be maintaining a tragedy.

If you don't set boundaries, subconsciously others realize you don't and that releases the floodgates of gall.

Those closest will get testy, seeing how much they can get away with. Shit tests galore, esp. with the toxic.

Those who do this are not self-developed, high-consciousness people. Animalistic, basic, evil.

They will always ask more, more, more until you hit bottom on them just cuz you didn't show who you are.

With users boundaries are even more important. They don't know anything from a lax liberal environment.

BE NICE

YOU'RE A SPONGE OF GROSS INVADERS

If not mimicking your gross invaders, you're always resisting/mad at em then that becomes a cancer.

Mike used to visit twice a month to debate me out of my views. I was so aggravated I got wrinkles.

If you're a conservative you know the frustration of debating liberals. I grew literally sick from it all.

So whether you're chiming in with them or resisting them, you take em on and it's in your nervous system.

It doesn't make it less legit cuz I experienced it as a social scientist.

See everything synchronistically as your unique destiny and you'll see it all fit together perfectly.

It will be terminal if not dealt with: ruin/tragedy. We must be on the offensive for the sake of all our progeny.

I hardly ever see him but he's there in case I need him. Older marriages are all about accommodation.

HANGOUT CULTURE WASTES TIME

Become a judge of character. If you tell em the problem and they keep busting boundaries, call the Sheriff.

Human beings run on patterns. You can tell if bad habits remain: if incorrigible, steer clear or go backwards.

I told him not to come to my house again. Weeks later he came with a gift only to create far worst bedlam.

If your boundaries are busted repeatedly you gotta cut him off completely and get outside help immediately.

If you don't, your boundary-setting is an empty threat and an abuse-magnet: reject and forget.

BE NICE

There are times you can't cut toxic people out. They have you over a barrel/know too much. Listen up:

Realizing you can't cut em out--boss or backer--is your impetus to getting independent [being on top].

So even though you're trapped, knowing that is the first step: establish a time period to work on that.

If you can't get away simply limit exposure to that person. Don't let anger in just start social engineerin'

If you've spent 20 hours a week with the toxic person, reduce it gradually until you're finally free.

As your time with him lessens your True Self emerges again free of the PAIN and CHAOS this person caused.

Your goal is to have a tranquil productive life with YOU in control, not having to suckup or put up anymore.

It's simple math: Cut his time in half, have half as much toxicity. Longing for him is thinking the other way.

SOCIAL TYRANNY GET AWAY FROM ME

Get away from me. I'm plenty nice to who I want to be but this is social tyranny.

Eventually you gotta give up, let em go and put your thoughts on someone else--you'll feel bliss.

You've gotta let em go cuz hanging on to someone who is hurting you is the SAME as enabling them.

The abuser--unhealed from his past--blames you. Let em go or he'll get his flying monkeys against you.

Just as quickly as she was nice she turned on a dime and showed her other side/couldn't believe my eyes.

BE NICE

You'll never reach your potential while letting others abuse you and blame you for things you haven't done.

Every time y.ou let em back in the cycle of violence gets a little bit shorter till it's bedlam or murder.

The little creep doesn't mean to be abusive and has a thousand excuses but just don't listen.

Melania on her beloved husband: "savvy, steely, ambitious, deliberate, plays long game".

He who writes for fools always finds a large public but life is short: never attend to the latest craze for support.

Stop resenting all the trouble they caused by realizing it was karma for all the trouble you caused darn it.

Her addiction caused em so much trouble then the whole world fell in on her in a chaotic muddle.

BEHAVIOR HAS CONSEQUENCES GOOD/BAD

We've got to see the karmic reflection in our actions. This is another way of saying: sin as CONSEQUENCES.

Solution for PTSD: You're in safe circumstances now so keep to the GRATITUDE for your now, don't go back then.

I stayed low waiting on the Lord. Then suddenly he removed the curse, brought me forth, doubled my worth.

It's important enemy sees the banquet laid out by the Lord. Coals on his head he sees his sins instead.

They saw you as a nothing or worse, now they see who you are in the Lord: a champion who comes first.

Her lunacy was a combo of broken attachment trauma and acting out another identity blocking her creativity.

BE NICE

You have everything one needs or could want--why go back to the trenches/what they did in your thoughts?

Life is in two parts: preparatory and success. When you're in bliss why go back/think about that past mess?

Yes they did horrible things but that's cuz people are horrible--the heart is wicked as written in the bible.

The more someone calls themselves "good", watch out. Jesus said NO one's good, only God.

I don't wanna read her stuff if she isn't godly, a lover of Christ. Why waste time, seek only the sublime.

I put people down just as I put Christ UP. It's entirely Christian to see the wild wickedness of crowds.

The narcissist always has his flying monkeys with him--crowds. Not only is it aggravating, he's no boss.

If women weren't yelling at me verbally they were gossiping/ruining my reputation [calumny].

DON'T FILL MY HOUSE WITH YOUR FRIENDS

Don't you dare fill my house with your friends. Come one by one with me vetting everyone and leave again.

People minimize the impact people have on people. The idea of putting em together helter skelter is evil.

While she hiked around she dropped her boyfriend off at my house to wait. That was a horrible imposition mate.

Andy yelled to Barney "get these women outa here" and that was ok in 1964 but now you're just a dam hater.

He came into my life and everything changed. From being a target I was finally free of society behind a fence.

BE NICE

Minimize/ignore me and I won't be around, period. I'm not gonna compete with your peanut gallery crowd.

Today I journey an hour to see my friend. It really warms my heart that I can speak and someone listens.

It hurts to be miscast cuz they don't have the smarts to see above the crowd/gas so put you in a lower caste.

ONLY A GENIUS SEES GENIUS

Only a genius can recognize a genius so how could those idiots understand? This was a mess to overcome.

They could lock me down a year and I wouldn't notice it. I've got food and internet, what's the problem with it?

But if I had to be locked down with a toxic abuser it would be miserable, as it was in the days of my early wars.

Life is in two parts: preparatory and success. When you're in bliss why go back/think about that past mess?

Why go local when you can go global? Because globalism makes you loco and the more local the more YOU.

Childhood PTSD is in its essence the loss of ability to connect to other people. Yes, I know.

Neglect and trauma in early life literally changes our brains and THAT'S why you act so strange.

Cue-trigger: In response to the cue we take off in bizarre reactions that even we don't understand.

Early trauma BLOCKS normal processes to distinguish bad vs. good people which we choose to "love" us.

CHILDHOOD PTSD

BE NICE

Childhood PTSD has devastating results: the ability to love yet unable to sustain a normal relationship.

Finally growing into healthy relationships can heal our PTSD from childhood: great news understood.

Most with PTSD have been hurt in their ability to connect. Is that you too friend? Socially I felt wrecked.

Emotional Dysregulation: An insult sends you into a tailspin propelling you to disordered eating.

Few therapists see bulimia/anorexia as EMOTIONAL illnesses but they are, leaking to the bio-basics.

The traumatized baby reaches for food then the adult decades later is a compulsive eater, robot-cued.

The disordered channel--anxiety calmed by food--is robot circuitry as the victim's a slave/rude.

Insult, devaluation = TRAUMA = food-seeking = anxiety quieted: all is well until system reacts again.

WHAT IS A REAL MAN?

Being a MAN is not about props--cigars, beards, pipes--but integrity and protecting us against thugs.

Go into your man cave and smoke a cigar/have a whiskey. Are you any more a man? This is all so phony.

The manosphere icon talks too much about sex. The REAL man has decency cuz he's an aristocrat.

The real man would never dream of talking of sex in mixed company. Like it's a feather in his cap--how loony.

ADDICTIVE DEVICES TO COMPENSATE

BE NICE

Some seek sex, some gamble, some gossip to quiet core pain--addictions vary--but it's all robot circuitry.

The clerk looks at her funny and it triggers her as a baby then thoughts of food take over life and body.

With bulimics [who everyone hates] it's double trouble as malnutrition combines with trauma = insane momma.

For 30 years in the desert wilderness I marched to a different drummer totally separate from culture.

You have the identified patient who's obviously "sick" then the others who can pass go but covertly ill.

As I proceeded in isolation when they came it was psychic devastation: how sick the culture was becoming!

Dignified men of substance--exemplars--never talked of sex mid-century. Copy them not the nasty.

DYSREGULATION AND ADDICTION

If not self-aware, you don't connect their actions with your triggered distress caving into your addictions.

"Caving in" is dysregulation where EMOTIONS are running the show not good judgement or what you know.

The dysregulated can't control how upset they are as their "inappropriate" behavior is off the charts.

Abusing/losing all control to food is an attempt to re-regulate emotions, putting focus back on self.

Food addict feels crazy in the mixed up world and her own personal "party" makes her time again orderly.

Re-regulate with life skills instead. Self-soothing positive self-talk, distractions, music--not being fed.

BE NICE

Loneliness and disconnection affects all but for us it's survival-related and gut-pain devastating.

Dysregulation brings total hell in one's life but re-regulation and fine routines ends all strife.

Childhood PTSD brings desperate extreme behaviors from total isolation to clinginess or fear they'll leave us.

Early trauma blocks our star as we cling to others, escape from them or try to control who they are.

When enmeshed thusly her own strengths aren't revealed nor her own problems exposed--it takes its toll.

The opposite extreme is pouring the identity into another as an extension of self, a budding tragedy.

Those who cling to relationships this way may get obsessed or when angry, even promiscuous!

Then there's more backlash and then relapse back into old scripts of a psychologically wrecked mess.

BACK INTO THE PORN TROUGH

The lady said: "I knew he was into porn again by his sudden sarcasm--it goes across the board."

He's acting differently so she checked his youtube history and sure enough, he's back to the porn trough.

Don't seek help from old discarders. Pray for calm and think: who are my true supporters in this chaos?

It starts out with "share my stories" on youtube, a gateway drug to harder porn then family feuds.

It's not just soft porn but Jerry Springer stuff, lowmindedness. In your mate? Don't allow this.

BE NICE

Compare his interest in the frivolous/silliness/nastiness to your great ancestors, always in their bible verses.

You DO have good models in your family--start looking way, way back. They were there, decency.

Because its disgusting: his interest in lowminded, nasty, evil things. He's not a boss, an underling.

It's a total repeat of what's happened times before. He's into porn again, I could tell by his lost allure.

Pornography is grounds for divorce cuz it's MENTAL adultery which is just as bad Jesus exhorted.

Pray: I feel betrayed, like someone stabbed me in the back/my world has gone black. God help me please, amen.

I must stay enigmatic at this dire time. I'm not gonna sink in my swill of looking to man for support, cryin'

The lady said: "I'm not gonna air our dirty laundry like I did last time--I gonna pray/gird up my loins".

When someone you trusted/relied on is looking/thinking about at those things it's a SHOCK/sickening.

The lady said: he brought me stability but recurrently I'd find porn and be devastated: betrayal insanity.

It's hard to tell with soft porn but you can tell from TITLES they're up to no good--but I want the Lord.

The same thing happened when I met you--in a TRAUMA from this ontologically fatal misinvestment.

NOT GONNA FALL APART AGAIN

I'm not gonna fall apart like I did two years ago, five years ago or God forbid when really immature/small.

BE NICE

I saw this all before, I worked this thru/cried my eyes out long ago, I've just been in another denial.

It's the Ontologically Fatal Insight that the world is **NOT** what you thought it was--and never was.

Even if it's "just" Jerry Springer level--isn't that bad enough? He's a **LOWMIND** that's the point.

I will **NOT** sink in my swill again with this thing cuz I know God always/forever wants the best for me.

I know one thing now, he's not worth worshipping. That's what it's been in denial about obvious things.

I exhort you to get out now before you really get hurt. If not by these antics then suicide or even worse.

The porn spirit is a **SUICIDE** spirit: it self-immolates in a shadow of death/anti-family--you should fear it.

What I'm falling apart about is the fact I forgave/forgot and assumed change recurrently just like that.

I don't hate him except insofar as I hate the devil--have **NO** contract with evil, I hurt when its near.

With age you get leery at how fast life can change but when it comes to certain things, get away.

HIS DO-NOTHING SPIRIT

Cuz it's a friggin' do-nothing spirit. It's not the beauty of a great old movie or lovely nooks in your home today.

I can't be one with **THAT**. That's such a severe undertow I wouldn't think of it--including not grieving it's loss.

I'm just fishin'. I don't know who'll eventually come to my aid or if I need it, I've a tough skin from hurtin'

BE NICE

Ha ha it's all a joke just to see who's listening or if anyone gives a dam about utterances from this dame.

Now that you know the scoop you can't make it happen. You'll be directed out by God/awareness alone.

I would disagree--I'd say Twitter IS the place to portray your feelings, not to potential discarders, see?

Heck, let it go into a book: that's why these things happen and always have. Chapters on nuts.

I KNEW it was happening from his growing sarcasm. A man just can't hide what's going on.

Awareness ALONE with God will give you escape. Don't do anything/start proceedings just pray and wait.

That's all I can say for now. I just gotta hurt all day/think about the meaning of these events around.

I can understand staying with him tho' he doesn't use a napkin but this other thing is too dam weird man.

Please God restore my reality to order and beauty out of this weird stuff all around me/him and on TV.

Secrecy is the abuser's weapon [think about that now]--but you can tell thru symbols something's off.

HAVE YOU BECOME A DETECTIVE?

Becoming a detective in a relationship is a sign of covert narcissism, as an empath senses contradiction.

You sense your whole world imploding while blinded by a covert narcissist, a wolf in sheep's clothing.

The covert narc milks his public image of being nice, good, loving, helpful and understanding.

BE NICE

Covert narcissist goes overboard with gift-giving "kindness" while mind says: something doesn't feel right.

Their gift-giving eerily congers up Strings Attached. They're weird man, an archetype of lowness.

He will **PRETEND** to be codependent: " I got my boss here" but it's all a ruse and clever cover up.

He's a psychopath for life meaning he'll never take the blame--it's always your fault--or feel shame.

Because of his mental adultery she relaxed boundaries and became more open/attractive to guys.

Pornography--mental adultery--is a relational crime. It's abuse and betrayal no matter what he's sayin'

SWEET MEAN CYCLE

The Sweet-Mean Cycle is the manipulative device by which narcissist keeps you around for supply.

He milks moments of goodness, pleasure, happiness and optimism to keep you in line with open supply.

As you live in bliss and he gives you everything **THEN** the switch into punishment as his sarcasm stings.

Having an underdeveloped emotional psyche, he splits: from very nice to very mean--sudden blitz.

Sweet-mean cycle is intermittent reinforcement like a slot machine. Sometimes he's sweet, sometimes mean.

Like a slot machine most of the time you get **NOTHING**--that's the addictive process/keeps you coming.

He'll give just enough to keep the longing going but never scratching that itch then **BOOM** he switches.

BE NICE

Narcs cheat cuz they feel a right to. Narcs are exploitative, entitled and lack empathy too.

They've a right to cheat--they're entitled to more. They easily get bored, need to have supply/an affair.

The likelihood of cheating from a lack of impulse control. He lunges at cute clerks he doesn't even know.

The narc is like a child in a candy store: when there's something in front of him he's lured.

In a relationship, cheating relieves his feelings of being chained--the narcissist's bad dream.

In the narcs mind, being in a committed relationship makes them inferior, less-than, boring.

Narcs seek sexual gratification not establishing true intimacy with their partner: not the same.

THEY CRAVE EXCITEMENT

They despise routine, crave excitement and bore very easily. Not a kindly house husband I'd say.

He was never true to anyone, the dirtiest one of the litter and the others know it despite his image of better.

Lord I'm almost dead, can I trust anyone on this ball of mud? Has it all been for naught? No, I found God.

Having an affair/porn/cheating introduces excitement and RISK--heck he knows she'll leave him for it fast.

A narcissist isn't always a Jim Dandy but someone who's been wiped out early and compensates dearly.

He despises the average, boring, mundane existence of what you see as lovely home life and happiness.

BE NICE

Even simple routines can cause depression in the narcissist, or being asked to put things away.

This guy won't compromise with you in creating a lovely home. It's always going to be a battle alone.

You're of the world, a slobbering idiot attuned in perfect conformity while saying you love liberty.

Deep inside your rebel's soul you're still influenced by the world to status-climb and come first.

I couldn't get him to do a thing--even tho' we'd discussed it, planned it and he even asked me to remind him.

For the above reasons cheating and having a double life are incredibly appealing to the narcissist.

Despite all he has to lose, being assured of that too, it just increases the high he gets by what he chooses.

The continual need for novelty increases as time goes on until it eventually/inevitably implodes on them.

INCENTIVE GONE, WIND FALLS COME

I never met a person with less incentive combined with a belief in wind falls sure to be coming to him.

One's into diligent work and order, the other's into no-rules disorder if he wants and still he's better.

He craves but loathes intimacy, his desire ebbs and flows at different times-- that's the only reason I find.

The narcissist can't tolerate your success nor truth. You're just an extension of his lazy sloth too.

He got you back and forth and round and round and up and down again--know you'll never win.

BE NICE

You gotta stop pretending and know there's no other way, just do what you need to do. Toni Braxton

I'd be so happy in my homelife and an atom bomb would hit by something I discovered about that twit.

Don't overreact cuz then you gotta apologize for that. You're aware now, events will roll out right.

Liberal feminists put themselves first, tolerate sin and they want open borders: let em all in.

Strong in self: don't need anyone, attraction. Weak in self: your social neediness is obvious son.

ATTACHMENT STYLE: APPROACH-AVOIDANCE

The narc's internal attachment style is approach-avoidance: I want commitment/it repels me.

He wants commitment but he's too special for a boring life like that and besides he deserves what he wants.

One reason narcs cheat/have affairs is they lack empathy/compassion for others, it's a bother.

Don't grieve too much for that alone is worshipping that clown, a repeat of so many other traumas.

The narc knows right from wrong but just doesn't have the capacity to care. Even if he did he wouldn't.

He does not have the ability to put himself in the shoes of the partner or understand her pain, again.

Narcissists are entitled, lack empathy and are exploitative. That explains why he did all that.

Because of the "three E's" cheating and having affairs is part of their genetic makeup, so buck up.

BE NICE

Overgiving is a clear sign of a narcissist who wants attention on him--a core need, so watch it.

The narcissist wears a plastic social personna which has great power over the dumbed down around ya.

You can't teach someone empathy--you either have it or you don't. If you don't it's just words, a blank.

Narcissists do not have the internal moral compass that keeps them from hurting/harming others.

Before you out him, understand: the narc is fiercely protective of his false self, so watch out.

He has a false belief of perfection and superiority and won't listen to anything contradictory.

It's a life or death situation when they're terrified of exposure. It's a grenade range for sure.

Since he lacks impulse-control, empathy or feelings of remorse this is a dangerous time for the victim.

MAINTAIN FALSE IDENTITY

To feel safe and secure in their make believe world they must have power/control over you/your words.

Gaslighting: If he thinks you're onto him he does everything to change your beliefs, you'll see.

He'll say your interpretation is wrong, your emotions are out of whack, you're overreacting like heck.

"He" is not the problem, it's YOU. He wants you to second guess your conclusions tho' it's obvious too.

He wants her to doubt herself by whatever means necessary so things go back to status quo.

BE NICE

In gaslighting phase they'll lay on lovebombing, thick. The constant "I love you" should make you think.

He wants to get you back under his spell ASAP and the way to do that historically is by loving you well.

Narcs are famous for projection: blaming you for the same things they're guilty of--recall it hon'

Betrayal leaves us powerless, helpless, vulnerable, wounded, damaged, broken--we can't trust.

Betrayal brings distrust in the goodness of his heart and we don't feel worthy of love or protection.

A drug/sex addict will betray that trust given him because his addiction is even MORE overpowering.

Betrayal triggers a sense we're not valued and that's the emotional reaction-- it destroys self-esteem.

Emotional dissatisfaction causes betrayal to regain admiration, validation, connection or intimacy.

Anger or loss is temporarily dispersed through an affair with no thought of the future consequences.

He's putting his own personal gratification/ego boost before the needs of those close to him.

NARCS HAVE NO EMPATHY

Since the narc has NO empathy and NO impulse control, betrayal of those closest is obviously inevitable. S

The narc gets bored easily and always looks for excitement not bothersome commitments.

The profound break in trust and intense emotions following it are like the death of a loved one.

BE NICE

For some, betrayal signals the END--the one thing the marriage can't bear, while others don't even care.

GRIEF is over the relationship AS it was known and the loss of trust that existed--we're sad/mixed up.

Grief has a finality: there is a sadness from lost expectation--you had a home together, in ruins.

Betrayal means a loss of security, loss of respect and loss of your "perfect relationships" ideal, now null.

"How could he do this to me" and "What else has he lied about" tops the roster of desperate thoughts.

Anger, resentment, blame, shock/bewilderment lead to many knee-jerk responses: don't let em.

Fight-flight reactions are triggered with a need to escape or defend ourselves against "hard life".

Emotional vertigo is a reaction to betrayal as the world is upside down causing dizzy nausea from shock.

Victims rationalize dissonance between caring vs. harmful actions--strengthening this "trauma bond"

Worse, right when we're hurt the culprit becomes loving and attentive to the wounds he's caused.

The danger of traumatic bonding lies in the impact repeated trauma has on us, often covert.

Repeated trauma = flashbacks and depression, followed by seeking nurturance from that guy again.

NO COMPROMISE TRUTH FOR PROMISE

To overcome trauma bonds, we can't "compromise truth for promise". Be aware of your state, love yourself.

BE NICE

It means **NOT** fantasizing how he'll change someday but being grounded in evidence he'll remain the **SAME.**

We must see his patterns as truly **PATTERNS** and that overcoming abuse could take decades.

When we've invested so much of a life with an abuser, building a life without him feels daunting.

TRAUMA BOND SYMPTOMS

Trauma Bond Symptoms are quite interesting as they fit the system and I will list them here:

1. Obsessing about people who have hurt you, though they are long gone. He's triggering this hon'

2. Continuing to seek contact with people whom you know will cause you further pain. Masochism!

3. Going "overboard" to help people who have been destructive to you: a people-pleasing fool.

4. Still being a "team member" when obviously things have gone destructive. Don't forget this.

5. Continuing attempts to get people to like you, though they are clearly using you. That was me too.

6. Trusting people again and again who have proven to be unreliable. Could this be more true?

7. Being unable to retreat from unhealthy relationships. Think back--it took a lot to release your grip.

8. Wanting to be understood by those who clearly do not care. Dear Lord I did this for years and years.

9. Choosing to stay in conflict though you could easily walk away. Think of those you tolerated honey.

BE NICE

10. Persistence trying to convince people there is a problem and they won't listen--none of em!

11. Remaining loyal to people who have betrayed you. Good heavens, I was a sucker to destroyers.

12. Being attracted to untrustworthy people. Trauma bonds wipe out discernment of good/evil.

13. Being forced to keep damaging secrets about exploitation or abuse. You're a sad recluse.

14. Maintaining contact with an abuser who acknowledges no responsibility. Not one iota--it's all you silly.

One lady said "I can forgive him cuz he's a dirty old man who will die soon anyway and I'll be free."

Just cuz you didn't make it with them, so what--forget em. You haven't met the link yet to stardom.

It isn't him you loved but the past inner snake pit he aroused, screaming/wanting to be resolved

NEVER REAL APOLOGIES

The narcissist will never give REAL apologies. It's sorry I got caught or that I inadvertently hurt you baby.

The narcissist doesn't hear you and doesn't WANT to hear you. He's not listening just blame-shifting.

A narc will NEVER provide you any sense of safety. It's not us against the world but me against treachery.

The narc knows better [good from evil] but chooses to do what he wants anyway, then it becomes habit.

The lady said "I couldn't get him to lift a finger--he just wanted to be a peeping Tom on the computer."

BE NICE

The narcissist will always blame-shift and gaslight. Don't allow this--it's HIS dirtiness, aye?

The narcissist KNOWS right from wrong but doesn't give a dam--he wants what he wants/you're to blame.

EVEN IF it's just Jerry Springer I still want it outa here--lowmindedness is a spirt I can no longer bare.

Men who are peeping toms on the computer [weird stuff] won't work around the home/lift a finger.

It was his SARCASM and sudden meanness that indicated to her he was into his weird stuff again.

The demon goes across the board but he's too stupid to realize his transparency/sneaks lose.

Fired up from weird sexual content then making her part of his dirty fantasy world—no more.

NO WEIRD STUFF!

You've a RIGHT to have standards as part of your core identity. Mine are high/that's how I got here see?

You've a RIGHT to prefer decency and having things NICE. Nothing off-color, no dirty jokes, nothing like that.

It was a horrible awful spirit you put me thru when you were here. I could sense it, a dark disorder.

He can leave and then watch all the weird stuff he wants. But not on my watch, I like things NICE.

He'll blame her rather than see how dirty he is. It isn't just porn but WEIRD STUFF, he has no lines.

He has no idea how disgusting this all is to a mature decent person. No lines, that's the reason.

BE NICE

What happened to him through his life? He's the dirtiest of the litter, none of his family acts this way.

You confront him and he's only concerned you spied on him not righteous remorse for what he's doin'

MOMMY SOFT PORN AND JERRY SPRINGER

Mommy porn has no nude pics and no explicit language but HORRIBLE concepts, can't you see that?

He knows right from wrong but chooses to do what he wants anyway, that's all. Let him go, walk tall.

Sarcasm, short fuse means he's into it again: lowminded weird stuff like Jerry Springer or mommy porn.

Soft porn victims boast there's no nude pictures/explicit language but the TITLES show they're garbage.

Tho' he was caught red-handed he insists you see it his way and besides he's moral and upstanding.

Instead of enumerating all his faults lets just put it all in the same bag: He Doesn't Have High Ideals.

He doesn't have high ideals and you're not on the same page. There's two excuses you can use.

Instead of enumerating all his faults and quibbling over that, say: I don't want him here/not a doormat.

I want a man with a natural revulsion against anything LOW: cheesy, silly, immoral, off-color, carnal.

It's a disrespectful SPIRIT in him which triggers FLASHBACKS in her of similar disrespecting.

I tried to make him appreciate the place but he couldn't--he's not into beauty just empty status symbols.

BE NICE

Just say "I like people with high ideals" and just like that you're rid of the heel.

NO NUDES/X LANGUAGE BUT STILL GARBAGE

No nude pictures and no explicit language but pure garbage. and maybe even the worst there is.

So he was good and helpful one day--so what? He vacillates and switches roles for supply.

You can't teach good manners. If someone's a jerk that's just the way it goes. Jenna Ryan

You either have good manners/respect for others or not. And if someone lacks EMPATHY they cannot.

If someone can't respect others don't waste your time trying to set boundaries, set up a wall quickly.

Have nothing to do with those people. You only want those at that level who can respect/love you too.

If it's someone healthy you can respond, talk and ask for change--you can REACT but not with a nut.

I lost my normal defenses that any animal in the wild would have. I let em all in as a good hostess.

Trauma bonds are when caregiver/romantic tie comforts the victim while also being the perpetrator.

The cure for trauma bonds is TRUTH over promise: he's not gonna change, he'll do it again I guess.

The more she rationalizes wide gulf between truth and promise the worse the trauma bond becomes.

The point is: he ain't gonna change. Stop living in fantasy land comfort or illusions of peace at any price.

OLD MEN'S BRAIN CONDITION AND SEX

BE NICE

The worse his brain condition became the more perverse his out of control actions, that's how it is.

As his condition worsened and the pressure rose his wife was mal-adapting through trauma bonds.

Thinking he'll change when it's obvious he won't actually strengthens the destructive trauma bond.

People have to be at a certain level to be able to respect and love us. Good manners are absent.

The dirty old man is weak, ya see--he doesn't have normal restraint of impulses and tendencies.

The good times are the glue of the system despite the bad times. Of course he's nice sometimes.

FLAKY NO-SHOWS

Flaky people who don't show up or answer back are disrespectful and should be avoided, yah?

A flaky no-show/call-back rips and tears at your self-esteem tho' at the time you ignored it, see?

I can't take flaky people who don't treat me with respect. No call-back/email-back and that's it chump.

You can't set boundaries with a flaky person or explain common courtesy, they have none.

Someone is either courteous and respectful or they're not. I'm not available for flakes, they can rot.

BANISH NO-SHOW FLAKES

It's not just a "no-show" but flakes display TOXIC behavior which is poison to the soul—I know.

BE NICE

If you continue relations with flakes who ignore you it damages your heart and self-worth.

You don't want flakes/their excuses in your presence cuz you deserve SO much more as God's precious.

He looked at me like I was the fool for daring to want him to be on time. Never, EVER deal with him again.

What is the message from someone cancelling at the last minute? Your time/feelings don't matter, get it?

It's friggin' RUDE to be flaky and not respond to people unless it's a F-U so that's how I take it from you.

Trauma Bonds: The one comforting you for the trauma is the one causing the trauma and it binds ya.

BOUNDARY-BUSTERS

If someone busts your boundaries constantly you may wonder: "why am I experiencing hurt feelings?"

Jezebel was a boundary-buster who was never taught discipline and had no manners--always imposin'

If you allow boundary-busters to impose, you're the bad term "doormat"--take it from one who knows.

Doormat behavior when people walk all over you: trauma bonds from the past wrecking the future.

There's a lovely moment in the life of every victim where they say NO MORE OF THIS and that is that.

Develop a lil' voice inside that rings an alarm when you're being mistreated/doormatted: go for it.

You must take ACTION against the actions of others who are invading your territory. Do it, it's FUN.

BE NICE

Standing up against invasion is the **ANIMATING CONTEST** to bring out your spirit, destiny and absolute best.

THEY'LL IMPOSE IF YOU LET EM

People will push the most absurd extremes of impositions on your privacy if you let them: must **STAND**.

Listen to your heart, **GUT** and take action. My gut hurt for years, my heart broken yet I laid down for them.

We all have humanity in us and humanity is desperately wicked. Buck up, ask forgiveness then forget it.

If you want me to express you Lord then give me the power to do it and I surely will, I have to.

Demanding respect when none is warranted: that's another pitfall of the liberal narrative.

Don't regress into your boring nice guy routine, please! It's so dam weak and we can **ALL** see it.

The Silent Treatment allows narcissist to take up a whole bunch of your energy in ruminations of him.

When they silent treatment you, go no-contact cuz that means they're no good. Jenny Ryan

The silent treatment is used by energy vampires to trip you up by closing you down, thinking of them.

It's very simple. The reason you went insane/acted like a lunatic was due to brain chemistry out of whack.

Thanks for your continued understanding/patience. You know who I'm talking about per chance?

It was a combo of malnutrition and living in a grenade range 24 hours a day = **TOTAL INSANITY**.

BE NICE

SILENT TREATMENT

We only have so much energy and the narcissist's silent treatment wipes it out in our worrying.

With the S.T. you must immediately go no-contact with no more wasted energy to wondering about that.

Go no-contact, low contact or grey rock with anyone who goes silent and you start to wonder about it.

When I went no-contact I instantly felt a lift as the energy vampire was taken off of me. Jubilee!

It's insidious, underhanded, secret. They're telling others to ignore you also, it's mean and a bagashit.

It's used as a punishment for not submitting or control of the victim. It's being cast out without protection.

If the narcissist has pathological envy he will use the silent treatment to control you--he's the enemy.

Never self-sabotage to get the abuser to stop using the silent treatment cuz it will just reinforce it.

Tension in a relationship can cause physical symptoms in the victim so don't cave into this system!

The narcissist will use the silent treatment if you're successful—female friends become full of bull.

When you set boundaries they'll use the silent treatment to get you back in line or put you down.

When I realized the silent treatment was a torture chamber it threw a new light on my sister.

EFFECT OF SILENT TREATMENT ON CHILD

BE NICE

Think of how the silent treatment causes a one-way relationship, on the begging end to twits.

You're in a fog, you're undifferentiated and idolize your parent. You please him or get silent treatment.

It causes the child or victim to doubt themselves and then become compliant unto submission: beta men.

If the only way to get em to talk is self-sabotage [so you won't be successful] it's chains, an energy-suck.

I heard my inner voice say "I don't like this" and finally, my higher self backed myself up: "leave this house!"

You should be assertive, not aggressive or submissive. You're asserting what you don't like, good.

LEAVE THE SNAKE PIT

You've a right to say this person makes you uncomfortable, you don't wanna go there, etc.

Stop chasing them as they're pushing you away. Stay firm, get alone, be with those who love you: ok.

You've invested years in the relationship but he's had his say and he doesn't care what you have to say.

Genius requires solitude. Be alone, that is the secret of all invention. Nikola Tesla

I left the snake pit and got into the position where no one is hurting me anymore: GATE/locked doors.

He went from sweet/kind to shallow, cold, petty, dishonest, disloyal: a narcissist in the flesh.

Don't forget he knows how to act empathetic, communal, familial--he knows ALL that stuff to get along.

BE NICE

The narcissist is a liar, deceiver, reprobate evil faker who doesn't care so why talk to him anymore?

THEY DIDN'T HONOR YOUR "NO"

Maybe they didn't honor your "no" or were threatened by your separate sense of self/disrespect shown.

If you don't honor your own "no" then you're going against your own instincts which will build/later blow.

People are nice when you meet em but so many complications times how many members in the system.

Anger is justified reaction to injustice. If blocked it builds to free-flying rage against who knows what.

Blowing up into a rage for no reason or passive aggressive stuff like constantly gossipin'.

Anger turned inward becomes depression or playing the victim card as we see in university's ragin'.

Connect your anger to the source. Realize anger is there to protect your rights--it's a good/vital force.

Learn your rights as a person and get in touch with who you are thru your anger--what's the reason?

LIBERALS HAVE DIRTY MINDS

States with most porn--like Utah--have the most plastic surgeons as wives compete with nude teens.

If you love cats and dogs they'll accuse you of bestiality. Liberals' minds are dirty/they can't love furries.

The major illness of the trauma-bonded is: thinking things have changed when they stay the same.

BE NICE

Liberal's minds are dirty having been desensitized through homo/pan sexuality and pornography.

They're practically ALL dirty--every one of them even the old ladies. Recall boomers got dirty in the 60's.

I know I did wrong spying on you/viewing your youtube history and I repent-- but at least now I know.

PORN IS CHEATING

Porn is cheating, Jesus said it. Mental adultery is the problem in this generation, block it.

When he clicked on that dirty thing his whole life changed--tho' it's just virtual he's deranged.

it wasn't nudity but "mommy porn", written smut of sister with brother, mom with son or who knows what.

Written smut is the worst because in a mental person it opens evil windows in the mind/it's disgusting.

It is clearly labeled "incest porn" in all titles--so if someone clicks on it you know they know.

I've written 100+ books, I gotta clear the decks. Giving all away [more blessed then selling], what the heck.

B.S.: I sense contradiction but am prevented from discussing it. Things don't add up so forget it?

PORN DEMORALIZATION WEAPON

Pornography is a sucking spirit as the wife loses all her senses though she's revolted as he denies it.

It wasn't just homosexuality that broke thru--it was PANsexuality, sex with anything/animals too.

BE NICE

If the globalists can demoralize us into this bottomless pit of evil they can control us—don't you see this?

Tom Jefferson even said: these principals will only hold for a moral nation. If not, forget it hon'

Its very sad for this immature cad because if the wife revolts over porn he'll try to commit suicide.

Then the worn-down wife of porn will say "he must love me cuz he tried to commit suicide over me."

Men focus on sex their whole life. With impotence they may substitute with porn tho' it causes strife.

The codependency model blames the poor spouse: she wasn't giving enough sex, it's all her fault.

The modern "victim" model says: his porn has nothing to do with her, he's just a dirty nasty feller.

If the forlorned wife of a porn addict sees a therapist who blames her for it she must immediately report it.

The entire solution to trauma bonds is realizing things haven't changed and will likely stay the same.

With sin you lose your liberties as you're handed over to the enemy, and with shame comes fatigue.

Globalists don't wanna save the 3rd world but bring us down to their level so there's no one to save em.

Inside I can hear women yelling at me: big sisters, mother, aunts, older, younger or screaming teens.

CODEPENDENCY OR VICTIM?

The codependency model that the wife causes/sabotages his alcoholism is PASSE and pure bull I'm sayin.

BE NICE

When a husband nurses her back/works to regain trust it's a trauma bond since he's the reason for it.

They look like little bugs with their eyes bugged out in extreme envy, wiping their mouths salivating.

One of the harshest effects of PTSD from early trauma is the inability to connect to people or love em.

DON'T CRAPFIT EVIL OFFSHOOTS

Don't "crapfit": settle for less cuz your self-esteem's a mess. Go for what you WANT nevertheless.

The terror I felt around new evil offshoots of the bloodline exactly reflected the original trauma and mind.

They went their own way and didn't care a crap what I felt. I wasn't even noticed or they hated my guts.

It was like another family was grafted in: the richness of true Christianity had all but been forgotten.

Great pastors, orators and churchbuilders in my ancestry were over-written by dam liberals for abortion.

Tho' I was a sinner [like everyone] I was totally disgusted with them and couldn't love em as "family".

Great orators and biblical scholars in Scotland I so admired--compared to these naive liars?

It was horrible being thrown together and they weren't one bit interested in our renowned ancestors.

When in their presence my gut ached [the solar plexus] and our incompatibility brought great distress.

Now if a schism like this can happen in your own family, just imagine the pain of miscegenation, truly.

BE NICE

I could never love these people because Christian principals far transcend any relation to them.

I can forgive [cuz that's what I'm supposed to do] but I can't forget the calumny and wanting me dead.

They're a buncha entitled brats born with a silver spoon in mouth who can't/won't discern evil from good.

Don't be a fool by ever leaving a nickel to a liberal. A good steward NEVER supports their kind of evil.

Jerry Lewis disinherited all five sons—think of that! Were they all dam liberals and he wouldn't reward demrats?

BE YOUR OWN SOCIAL ENGINEER

As your own social engineer you can come up with creative ways to limit exposure/reduce total load, for sure.

Seeing things this way keeps you in control in a secret game we play. Solve all people problems this way.

If you're dependent financially a sudden breakup may not be smart or there is violence: so gradually depart.

Hopefully in the long run you're working to solve the rage but for now, secret plans to gradually disengage.

As you gradually disengage from toxic complication, add more positive people and now things are changing.

Positive additions can be digital: Add youtube mentors and those are your positive associations--wow!

Someone who inspires you on youtube is a virtual associate and that is as powerful as a friend or classmate.

If you can't cut the toxic right out, a virtual friend can PULL you out in the meantime to get things going.

BE NICE

Why were you in that situation in the first place? It can always be worked back to early life of the ace.

That's how you nip it in the bud in the future: Drill deep to your core, cry it out then go forward.

No more reason for self-consciousness honey since no one cares or ever thinks about you anyway--you're free.

Just like previous discoverers I ask: Why was I chosen to be the vessel for this marvelous work and wonder?

When it hits the mark I always think "wow this was so much easier than I thought." God is so good.

HIX POLITIX

The democratic party needs to be destroyed before it destroys the country. Mike Adams

Our rulers really appear to believe that the West belongs to whoever shows up. Jared Taylor

White people are told if they want a safe future for their own kind, they are scum--but other races can.

These invaders hate us for what we have built and despise us for letting them take it away without guilt.

It's not racism, it's evil vs. good: Evil has always existed but racism is a made-up term and misunderstood.

There is modern racism against white people. Even whites hate themselves riddled with guilt /calling em evil.

The left says only the powerful can be racist--powerless blacks killing whites is dismissed/doesn't exist.

After all he's done for our country, you talk stupid stuff like this? Ban me, I couldn't care less.

BE NICE

Stupidities: Old hippies from the sixties are all the same, many in their eighties saying things so inane!

In an effort to help small businesses Paypal no longer charges back when we don't get our purchases.

In Europe we've moved from the beginning of the END to the middle and it's happening here too friends.

It's BIGGER than Trump, it's the Deep State.

STUPID STUFF BY STUPID PEOPLE

Joan Baez song "Nasty Man" is a stupid song by a stupid woman. Old hippies from the 60's will soon be gone.

In the decline of civilization there's a stage of self-hate and even welcoming barbaric predators at the gate.

At this stage there's a flood of outsiders who take over. Tho' not inferior they are different from insiders.

As culturally different they form their own communities for their own interests not the nation as a whole.

The newcomers flood in at the tail end of empire when it's still strong but as it falters old grievances are on.

Newbies are loyal only in times of stability. As it atomizes and divides warring groups predominate over state.

Tension between groups increases/spills out to the streets. Punishments are lessened/creeps are freed.

Heroes of the declining society are singers, actors and athletes--not statesmen, academics or philosophers.

Romans demanded free meals and games or bread and circuses and went into ruin, vulnerable to crises.

BE NICE

At this point are cries for a bigger state to satisfy material needs for y'all who are so busy playing sportsball.

Ballgame enthusiasts are grown men uninvolved in local communities kicking balls to the howls of other men.

SPORTSBALL IS ALL

Sportsball and players are then elevated to a national obsession with decreased interest in protection.

As civilization further declines there is a complete abandonment of sexual morals until it's total.

The collapse of strong state/empires: Seven great empires have disappeared in the last 100 years.

Monopolies don't last nor do empires: Ottoman, Austro-Hungarian, French, British, Japanese, Soviet, German.

I've read 1000 history books and that is the one pattern flowing thru history: flourishing then ruin.

History fascinated me beyond belief. The patterns were so obvious and this evolution worked like a machine.

It's an emotional hookup, sportsball-obsessed cowardly submissive, low testosterone PC femme society.

While we're being transformed by floods of invading culture's we're told to constantly apologize.

While we're being transformed by floods of invading cultures we're to apologize to the vultures.

As EU attempts Empire via economic unity, it fails miserably as groups have long rival memories.

As they add historically hostile cultural groups they'll be fractured and bread and circuses won't help.

BE NICE

BOTOX AND OTHER DAM SCAMS

Don't use bad words just cuz they're popular. Be better than them, find choice words not just "fu*kem".

Tho' botox seems less drastic than a facelift, it's not. A facelift is permanent and your face won't rot.

Botox: You need forty years to prove something is safe. I'll be dead and gone, but come on...

Dentists dissuade dentures to keep putting crowns back in. Surgeons dissuade facelifts so botox keeps you comin'.

Women should want permanence not temporary fixes. A facelift not injections of chemical experiments.

I don't mind cooking but with continuous revelation I don't have time. A good cook would be sublime.

BOTOX: Hey you could live/flourish beyond 90 if you weren't shooting shit under the skin honey.

If immuno-suppressive botox flattens the face. As immunity attack foreigners, that's always the case.

If immuno-suppressive botox flattens the face. As immunity attacks the foreign that's always the case.

Plastic surgeons are responsible to read up on it. It's staring in your face by putting botox in the search.

I love pizza and Michelle Obama said pizza is a vegetable.

Botox is a dam scam that has to be done forever again when all you needed was a lift—no injections.

I've been writing for twelve hours and am winding down with delicious music expanding mind so far!

BE NICE

Botox is pushed as a cheap alternative to a lift but you gotta keep doing it while the lift is permanent.

Within 2.5 years you've paid enough for a lift but now you gotta keep going: 4 grand a year while muscles atrophy.

DON'T GET ON THAT WHEEL

Don't do it--don't get on that wheel. Plastic surgeons push the cheap substitute but it's dangerous dude.

The average lift costs ten grand, ten years of injections $40,000--no wonder they're pushin' em.

With Botox you **GOTTA** keep it up or you'll be uglier and more wrinkled than heck--avoid this setup!

Encephalize--elongate the head [aristocratic]--but when immunity reacts against botox it **FLATTENS** it.

You want enchephalization--elongation of planes, lines, angles--not de-encephalization: a **SQUARE!**

Anything you eat, drink or use could trigger your autoimmune and you'll look like a commoner.

Botox is pushed as cheap alternative to a lift but in the long run it's **FAR** more expensive and dangerous.

Ten years of botox is forty grand. Could that be why they're pushing this dangerous trend?

I'm not one bit offended that he never reads my work, couldn't care less and prefers cowboy movies.

GRATITUDE IS AN OPENER

It can change your life just being thankful. Thank and praise Him for everything and life becomes full.

BE NICE

Just being thankful runs the devil off but **NOT** being so changes everything so now he's on top.

Because you did not serve the Lord with gratitude you shall serve your enemies. Deut 28: 47-8

Use your faults, use your defects; then you're going to be a star. Edith Piaf

Another way of saying: success comes from failing to the top. Don't get stuck in remorse, go/never stop.

It isn't the butcher we should know but the baker and candlestick maker when electricity is rare.

Just not into steak and eggs, sorry. It's not my thing, just a little fish/shrimp in afternoon lowcarbing.

I can't store it any longer--I gotta clear the decks. Get rid of everything holding me to earth and it's hex.

Toxic shame comes from being improperly mirrored early--fogging the true self which is under it, buried.

Why did she present that crap in her art? We swim in muddy waters, with no morals that's what we are.

Men hope women never change and they always do. Women hope men will change and they never do.

I didn't hang with them, they imposed on me and I was overwhelmed/too weak to lay boundaries.

Flying monkeys is when suddenly all his/her friends are mad at you for seemingly no reason: see this.

They were so weak they always had an entourage--an army against you from their envious backbiting.

THERE IS NOTHING IN THEIR HEAD

BE NICE

They could never write like this since they don't have a thing to say. Sad: the drought of latter days.

Why am I an endless spout? Cuz I learned about myself, tamed my instincts and got the bad out.

Because she was destroying herself she destroyed anyone near her. Dirk Bogarde on Judy Garland

I always take everything for the DAY and never look back. There's no point cuz it's gone. Dirk Bogarde

It's not that I'm good-looking but that I have a quality inside me that orders the face. Dirk Bogarde

I prayed God would give me something to do so He put a Creative Act inside me and it took decades too.

Van Gogh and Gauguin argued constantly about painting. I don't like community, I'd rather be solo writing.

THE END

You don't lose friends just undercover haters. Real friends are never lost and frenemies should be goners.

What is success? It isn't money, fame, positions, status, popularity/high-rate but ONE thing: a locked gate.

A skid row bum has NO privacy. Privacy is the greatest commodity and it's true success/being happy.

Losing privacy/hedge of protection was my Ph.D. in the Streets [taught me more than a library of books].

My greatest success was moving from the past, finding the safest place with a fence and locked gate.

I'm sure your friends are great but that's not that point--I have a right to vet. It's my house, not yours kid.

BE NICE

Stop thinking about the war before you had a locked gate. That was just your lesson seeing the need for it.

What are you gonna do, go yell at someone in a rest home? Eventually we just forgive/let it go.

God washed the past clean but you still feel shame--that's a reflection of the trauma from which you came.

Rather than rationalizing it/searing conscience and tucking it away--face it/end it by seeing it's **NOT** ok.

HOW TO RID TOXIC MEMORY

It's time to stop voices in your head. This is all from being a sitting duck but now you're above it all.

God said "we've won those battles--forget em. Now let's concentrate on the talents and self-expressions."

Don't waste time remorsing over toothless losers from the past. This is giving **THEM** the power lass.

Psalms says God broke the teeth of the ungodly. When I saw him again he had no teeth and was weaselly.

FAME is above all that crap you're worrying about. Losers from the past--close that door and go forward fast.

God said "stop fighting old battles in your head--it's a battlefield of the devil, don't you know that?"

Fame is being above the inferior herd putting you down out of pure spite and jealousy on the way up.

Thank you Shane and Chris for teaching me by example how **BAD** people can get, I will **NEVER** forget.

Jesus is like a magic carpet ride, flying away from the dreary past and letting it **ALL GO: ALL AGLOW.**

BE NICE

To rid noxious memory I visualize leaving earth. In death it all disperses anyway like it never occurred.

They treat aging like it's a disease. Don't put up with evil projections--you're at your top/will please.

Here's the gist: the best saints WERE the worst sinners--that's why you gotta leave old areas/systems.

Don't hate em just be glad you're rid of em. You obviously had to learn a lesson or they wouldn't be a problem.

THAT OLD ERA ERASED IN HISTORY

That whole era when blocked by the devil is now blacked out in memory having been ERASED in history.

Dirk wrote lady for eight years every single day, though they never met nor ever thought of it again.

The whites were mean but the others were worse. When I was Maria Civetta I experienced this curse.

Regarding the bad past, God buried it in the deepest part of the ocean and put a sign: don't go fishin'

If at death all these crazy memories disperse like nothing why not NOW get rid of em/success needs room.

Drop the self-disgust and instead feel sorry for yourself--for what you went thru to be the magic elf.

I had nothing but people problems since the day I was born but with a locked gate, it's heaven galore.

GOD A DANGEROUS ENEMY OF SIN

God is our friend but he's the most dangerous and deadly enemy the sinner has--could mean the end.

BE NICE

When God was angry with me I had holes in my bucket--losses, accidents, enmities, failure, uglies.

Liberals say God is all-loving--that's a deadly lie. He loves when we're good but our sin makes Him cry.

People fear everything but God when He is the One we SHOULD fear for we'd be way less flawed.

By deeds of the law NO flesh will be justified before God--it's something we can't do anything about.

When it gets like Nazi Germany with 99.99% thinking similarly it's best to be alone--think of it that way.

I feel grateful for all God's given me after a extended period of trials seemingly without remedy.

INVASION INTO ISOLATION

Living in isolation in the desert I was a nation without a fence whenever imposed on by the dense.

They musta thought I was lonely or bored way out there or they'd come cuz they liked country/felt freer.

But after being alone and LOVING it, every arrival was pure hell and I thought only of ESCAPING it.

Even thinking of it brings PTSD symptoms of how I was terrified of invasions of gross creeps, just sayin'

But that's all over now, my Ph.D. in the Streets. Many are dead cuz that's what happens to losers mis-led.

30 years in a small town taught me a library of books about gossip/slander/calumny/WOMEN.

I knew they were too dumb to understand me--I was strange to em and being targeted like in Psalms.

BE NICE

After years of persecution, hatreds, flying monkeys and triangulations marriage put it all to an end.

Marriage was like leaving the dark pagan chaotic world and coming into a beautiful walled garden.

I couldn't trust ONE female and I couldn't trust ONE man and that was my life until marriage came.

It is more blessed to give than to sell. Donated $8000 worth of new flooring--feel so good I could yell.

PH.D D IN THE STREETS

To get my Ph.D. in the Streets I had to go thru a war in the devil's playground. Now I know it all, well-armed.

The social generation is entirely non-discerning. They let anyone into their homes and even sleep with em.

Neighbor had an average of 8 cars there before. Social is her whole thing so lockdown is pure torture.

When memories intrude, think "that was my education to get to where I am now" then quickly let em go.

To make me miserable/kill me a sister laid evil seeds with everyone in town before I arrived, no jive.

To make me miserable/kill me a sister made all her friends hate me and I couldn't figure out why, oh me.

Dad said though I was endlessly clever I was born in hot water--a generational curse or whatever.

See the past achetypically. These weren't actors they were bad archetypes because we were lower.

ARCHETYPICAL LEVELS

BE NICE

Our trials reflected our archetypical level--we were caricatured humans not superior specimens.

The more people reject the more you know you're close to the final mark. Success is coming, look up!

As you raise your archetype thru purity you're in dysynchrony with those beneath thee.

Because you've had nothing but trouble you expect to always be in hot water--not true, it's over.

Finally rid of the evil "helper" I got the job done. Finally rid of evil "friend" I felt loved eternally to the end.

RECAP ON LIBERAL AREAS

There's no more reason for self-consciousness since in this generation no one's thinking about you Miss.

To get to here I suffered many years. That's what happens if you don't learn it from your parents.

In the sixties everyone loved the Rat Pack who drank openly and copiously on stage, starting a rage.

Just as Blanche in the Golden Girls made sluts look cute, the Rat Pack made drinking into high class cool.

Your boundaries must have teeth or users will sense your idle threats and push you to the max.

You gotta draw the line somewhere. No cuddling before we're married, I swear.

Cannibus opens windows in the mind. Are these distortions? No just new rooms in your mansion. BUT:

Living in a liberal town the losers wouldn't leave me alone and I didn't get peace till I moved and calmed down.

BE NICE

I'm telling you how to get Trump. He promised us a wall for 18 months and lied about it. Ann Counter

For a president who ran on closing the borders this is the worse open borders we've ever had. Ann Coulter

HEALTHY MINDEDNESS

It's true--I always needed the carbs, sugars and fats together for high-powered breakfast I wager.

Europeans are very beautiful sensuous happy people so there must be a reason for bakery first then fish later.

High carb/fat/sugar: get that high-powered jet engine going! BOOM! Then slow burn to a little fish in the afternoon.

It's how **BREAKFAST** is always done. High sugar, starch, fat and other delicious things like that then **FAST**.

EAT AS THEY DID IN HISTORY

Dad was handsome/slim/sleek until 90 and each day he had toast [1/2" butter on it], jam, bacon, eggs, coffee.

Mom was skinny and loved pancakes with maple syrup and lotsa butter but then she didn't eat again either.

The trendy green-juicers for breakfast look chunky/haggard compared to the bakery eaters then fasters.

Cease judging food by vitaminerals/start judging it by **SATIETY POWER [SP]** where you can go many hours.

Fasting is the **MOST** beneficial beyond food. So eat then **DON'T** eat cuz you ate dense calories/satiety power.

I need those carbs in the morning to brighten my day later, well glycogen-supplied so I am **SATISFIED**.

BE NICE

Go ahead, eat all the no-carb meat you want--now check out your eye-bags which are so pronounced.

You have eye-bags cuz your kidneys are clogged after the brainwash about the beauty from no-carbs.

I've noticed if I have music on the dogs don't demand to go out and play ball so much, just at lunch.

Taking my high-end Vitamin C herbs in grape juice. High as a kite, love the mornings, no need for coffee.

Living on juices and powerful herbs. No more fruits and vegetables covered in bio-sludge, what a curse.

What soothes acid reflux? Ice cream. What do you feed kids after tonsils removed? Ice cream, see?

EUROPE: BAKERY THEN FISH

Morning: High carb/sugar/fat meal. Then two juice meals with powerful herbs: high as a kite/millionaire feel.

ONE digestive burn is great but two misses the boat and I'm fatigued/low rate. Just JUICE later I say.

BEST C: sea bucktorn/cubinge/amla berry, acerola, rosehip, guava/pine needle/watercress/orange peel.

I take my BEST C in grape juice first. Then I take my LIVER and KIDNEY herbs in 2 meals with juice.

Liver: dandelion chanca burdock nettle rtichoke black cumin schizandra uphleurum, andrographis, orange peel.

Kidney: Nettle asparagus chiana magnesium, Uva Ursi, pectin hydrangea cinnamon juniper/ emon peel.

If feel so good not to have to digest. One meal is ok but more is a real pest. Just juice, herbs, music, rest.

BE NICE

There's a life phase where digestion is your greatest enemy. There's a budget-
-we've limited energy.

One digestion burn, fine. But two: immune response to antigen as a foreign
invader and I wanna die!

MAKING YOU SICK THRU MEALS

They made me sick from the outset by forcing a sit down to three meals a day.
From the beginning, ok?

Just as one meal barely digested they'd make me eat again. It was such a drag
and I knew it back then.

When mom left a few days I'd fast and be SO HIGH feeling like it was a
Saturday. God's trump card was ok.

Once break-fast is done I'm "off" for the day anticipating God's miracles. But
if I eat, life becomes folderol.

Grace Jones at 71 stays young by eating 240 oysters a day. Whatever it is, it's
your own personal way.

Mine is not eating past 6 am. or life is HELL and who knows why--it's genetic
I've been told.

What happens if I eat twice: burping, acid reflux, feeling miserable/stuffed,
lowminded and it all sux.

Don't use potentially charming nooks as "catch-alls" for all your crap.
Eliminate 80%, now be delighted.

FORGET DIET DOGMA JUST FAST

And I'm not gonna eat a buncha boring fruits and veggies for breakfast, either.
What I eat ain't your bother.

I want a HIGH fat, sugar and carb breakfast like i always had as a child getting
fired up at the trough.

BE NICE

I'm not worried about the loss of vitaminerals since I'm getting the best in my herbal juice meals I attest.

Digestion/assimilation/elimination is 85% of our energy--why waste it? I'm so high I wouldn't think of it.

I'm so happy with digestion behind me. It's such a pill, a drug/chore/downer I don't wanna go there, see?

ONE meal--breakfast--and there's no problem. I enjoy the mornin' then fly into the aft-fast dreamin'.

It doesn't matter what I eat for break-fast my body takes what it needs then heals from the fast.

EAT WHAT/ALL YOU WANT THEN FAST

I eat pastries, corn on the cob, lotsa sugar, home made pizza or shrimp/salmon in butter or whatever.

I'm 5'3" and weigh 102 lbs.--cuz the aft-fast makes everything perfect but if 2-3 meals it wouldn't.

In the last century Americans had the BIGGEST breakfasts, a real production/most important.

The skinniest specimens ate loads of butter, honey, bread, bacon/sausage, eggs, pancakes for breakfast.

That's the time you're in the pad man, the rest of the day you should be working the fields or something.

It's only the new age beta couch potatoes who stay in the home at the frig all day long. Weak weasels.

You have your big breakfast then you're "off" to a higher creative world all day: prosperous and savvy.

if you wish dinner-only that's your prerogative, I'm just telling you how they did it then, the tough men.

BE NICE

The tough men never knew if they'd be eating again, life was bigger than that when taking action.

You have your break-fast cuz you don't know if you'll be eating again and it doesn't matter if you do.

SATEITY POWER NOT VITAMINERALS

I don't eat for entertainment anymore. I eat to fuel the tank so I won't be hungry all day and night.

Fasting is higher than food when it comes to energy and healing so that's what I'm doing thru SATIETY.

When a cowboy eats it must be the most calorically dense foods cuz that may be it. Levoy Finnicum

Yah we cowboys have to carb-up in the morning with lotsa fat too. It's about satiety and hard work ya' know.

Have an ice cream sunday too--with caramel on top! You'll see it all goes thru, it's all irrelevant.

The body's so efficient with daily fasting it'll correct all wrongs and maximize energy more each day.

Foods were judged by SATIETY POWER. That's old Americana with citizens working every hour.

I've grown to love our neighborhood bakery. That's my morning fuel and they say I'm really pretty.

In the 80's even shrimp cocktail or salmon was called "cholesterol danger"-- that's why we're fat sir.

All that fat and sugar together is a rocket launcher then it's a slow burn of fasting satiety much longer.

There may be a candida bloom, you may even expand but it all deflates back down thru the daily fast.

BE NICE

Have your apple strudel or cinnamon roll with lotsa butter now fast with ease, you won't wanna eat later.

We need/run on glucose for energy but we also need fat for brain and satiety: bakery does it for me.

I've noticed if I have music on the dogs don't demand to go out and play ball so much, just at lunch.

In my **DEEP FEMALE VOICES** playlist I've got the best in the business expressing my deepest thoughts.

GLOBAL BLOCKS TO SUCCESS

Successful people fail their way to the top. Write things off, give stuff away, begin again and **NEVER** stop.

The benefits of giving things away far exceed those from selling them. Give and God multiplies em.

LOW OXYGEN is how they're gonna bring in world government and forced inoculation.

5G AND VIRUSES: The root cause analysis of what's **REALLY** going on is the Master Plan.

They wanna make us so sick that we can't live without the transhuman movement--that's all, get it.

Depopulation idea started 100 years ago, got discredited under Hitler and went underground: Bill Gates.

The vaccine is the depopulation kill-switch, covid 19 is just the device to make it forced on us.

Die or go to a new world? Die or just exit one to open to another much better, away from liberals?

They think they're saved from mere religious activity. Get-togethers and boring meetings etc.

BE NICE

The Party of the Ass demands we import a new electorate. It's not ceasing and we've had it.

It's in my DNA to want things utterly orderly. Everything in it's place, a place for all, everything polished.

Disorder and chaos is so low-class it makes me depressed. Superfluity, nonessentiality, a mess.

AFFINITY OR MISERY
AGELESS CORNUCOPIA
AMERICA AWAKE!
AMERICA'S DAFT ERA
ARTS OF PALEO FASTING
AUTOPHAGY ON CHEATERS
BACKSTABBING NEUROTICS
BETRAYAL TRAUMA
BOOMERS AND BROKENNESS
BOOT ON NECK
CHAMPION GUIDES
COMMIE NUTHOUSE
COMMIES
COMMUNIST SPIRIT
CONTAGION OF MADNESS
CONTAGIOUS MADNESS
CULTURE CLASH BASHED
DAFT LEFT
DAILY FASTARIAN
DAM RATS
DIVERSITY IS CRUELTY
E-RACE WHITE
EVIL FREAKS (Beyond Gross)
THE END OR A BEND?
FEMALE BULLIES AND FEMI-NAZIS
FEMALE CARNALITY
FEMALE DUMB DOWN
FEMALE POWER DRIVE
FEMINISM AND RUIN 1 & 2
FIX FOR MISFITS
FOOLS & TRAMPS
FREEDOM SPEAKING
FRENEMY ENABLER
FRENEMY LIAR
FRENEMY THIEF
FRENEMY TRAITOR
TRENEMY TYRANT
GENIUS IS HELD DOWN
GLOBALISLAM
GOD USES THE FLAWED
HAZE OF THE LATTER DAYS

AUTHOR BIO

Karen Kellock Ph.D.

Ph.D Political Psychology, UCI 1976
Post-Doctoral: UCI Medical School
Department of Psychiatry
Grants NIMH, NIAAA

Ph.D. dissertation "A Systems-Theoretic View of Pathologic Interaction" made an early mark as the "Wife of the Alcoholic Syndrome". Postdoctoral research at UCI Medical, Dept. of Psychiatry on the systems surrounding pathology on NIMH and NIAAA federal grants: *The Contagion of Madness: The Psychology of Neurotic Interaction and Pathological Systems*. Therapy tool Therapeutic Playwriting introduced the play *Mary and Murv: Gruesome Twosomes in the Alcoholic Marriage*. She taught Abnormal Psychology and Pathological Systems Theory at UC and CSU campuses and developed "the Debris Theory of Disease" in five books and website: (www.karenkellock.org): *Champion Guides, Daily Fastarian, Just Skip Dinner, Arts of Paleo Fasting, Ageless Cornucopia. Manual for Superior Men is a* pick-it-up-anywhere book that you can't put down (20,000 Kellockialisms) and ever on your desktop it should be found (or this Ebook for superior wordsearch of new jargon).

www.ingramcontent.com/pod-product-compliance
Lightning Source LLC
Chambersburg PA
CBHW061719250726
48657CB00002B/675